More Hidden Crete

A Notebook

By Richard Clark

First published in America and Great Britain 2017
Copyright © 2017 by Richard Clark
Book design and Layout © 2017 by Cheryl Perez
Cover design © by David Richardson 2017

ISBN – 13: 978-1545176832
ISBN – 10: 1545176833
www.facebook.com/richardclarkbooks

By the Same Author

The Greek Islands – A Notebook
ISBN: 9781466285316
ASIN: B005O044PS

Crete – A Notebook
ISBN: 978-1500761646
ASIN: B008N9ES1M

Rhodes – A Notebook
ISBN: 9781483971285
ASIN: B00DJI8TDU

Corfu – A Notebook
ISBN –9781492877097
ASIN – B00J22FOTY

Richard Clark's Greek Islands Anthology
ISBN: 9781497575788777
ASIN: B00K1X13AU

Hidden Crete – A Notebook
ISBN –9781534999367
ASIN – B01LZN8JIC

Praise for Crete – A Notebook

'I was really surprised and delighted by the book. I read every word. The author is a fine writer and describes the island vividly. He travels around the island in a clockwise direction, writing short essays as he goes, which are a mix of personal memoir, history, and an evocation of place. He really does capture places well.'

Mike Gerrard, author of *AA Spiral Guide to Crete*

'I love the way Clark writes, it is personal, it is human and deceptively simple.'

Sara Alexi, bestselling author of *The Greek Village Series*

'Unsurprisingly, travel literature constitutes the vast majority of my reading these days. In examining other writers' style and content, I have become accustomed to dipping in and out of work. The extent to which I have been unable to put Richard Clark's book down is a tribute to its compulsive readability.'

Emma French, travel journalist *www.phileasfrench.com*

Praise for The Greek Islands – A Notebook

'Clark is particularly good on the colours, flavours and scents of Greece. He has got under the skin of the place in a way few outsiders have been able to.'

Mark Hudson, winner of **Somerset Maugham Award, Thomas Cook Travel Book Award, Samuel Johnson Prize**

'This is a beautifully written book, it is an education in itself and I found myself so much the richer in having read it.'

E.J. Russell, bestselling author of ***Return to the Aegean*** and ***Aegean Abduction***

'What I liked most about the book was that it was personal and with that came an honesty, no wrappings, no embellishments other than descriptions of Greece itself. I would recommend this book both to people who have never been to Greece as well as to seasoned travellers. It was a joy.'

Sara Alexi

'My library contains almost all of the noteworthy books about Greece and her islands and this will be a welcomed addition. I will place it next to my collection of books by the late and great Patrick Leigh Fermor, because I think Richard Clark's writing is as close to Fermor as we will ever come again.'

Aurelia Smeltz, author of ***Labyrinthine Ways, A Lone Red Apple***

Praise for Rhodes – A Notebook

'Richard Clark writes with great authority and a deep affection for his subject, which comes from his long association with Greece… This is an excellent read.'

Marjory McGinn, bestselling author of ***Things Can Only Get Feta, Homer's Where the Heart Is, A Scorpion in the Lemon Tree***

'Well worth a read - and don't miss the Crete book too. The book made me long to see some of the places he describes so lovingly.'

Jen Barclay, bestselling author of ***Falling in Honey, An Octopus in My Ouzo***

'This is a book that has been written with great care and love and it shows. An absolute pleasure.'

E.J. Russell

'There is poetry in Richard Clark's words and through his eyes. I recommend anyone missing Greece, visiting Greece or just wishing they could go to Greece to take a look!'

Sara Alexi

Praise for Corfu – A Notebook

'This is another delightful book in the Notebook series of guides to the Greek islands. Richard Clark has an easy, relaxed style and his journey around Corfu feels like spending a leisurely few days with an old friend in a favourite location, enjoying long meals in seaside tavernas or enjoying dramatic moments on a beachside terrace while a thunderstorm rolls in from the mainland.'

Marjory McGinn

'Richard Clark's descriptive prose instantly transports the reader there to these mellow and beautiful places. You know you are onto a good thing when the way an author writes makes images that remain in your mind long after you have finished reading. Buy this book, feast on it, then visit the places that have already become your friends.'

E.J. Russell

Praise for Hidden Crete – A Notebook

'Crete was my first love out of all the islands of Greece but this book has made me realise how little of the island I really know, and how much more there is to explore. To say it was a delightful read would be an understatement. There are others in this series but this is the latest and easily his best.'

Sara Alexi

'*Hidden Crete* gives a very personal, and positive view of fabulous places to visit when you want to get away from the most obvious tourist spots on Crete. For me it was like meeting old friends'

Yvonne Payne, bestselling author of
Kritsotopoula: Girl of Kritsa

For Pete

Acknowledgements

More Hidden Crete – A Notebook is my third book about this magical island. As with my previous volume *Hidden Crete*, I hope that I have written about places and things that otherwise may slip through the net, and that travellers who want to make discoveries in the backwaters of the island will be inspired to explore off the beaten track themselves. For those familiar with the places and experiences described here, I hope it brings back happy memories. The book is part memoir, and as such if in some instances I have misremembered any detail I can only apologise.

This series of books has found more success than I could ever have imagined when I set out to write about Greece and her islands. I am particularly indebted to authors Mark Hudson, Marjory McGinn, Sara Alexi, John Manuel and Yvonne Payne for their continued support.

Thanks must also go to the writer Evi Routoula and translator Stella Chatzi for always being there with help when I am struggling with my research, which is frequently, as so often in Greece there are one hundred different answers to a single question. When things are open to interpretation, any perception is purely mine. The names of some people who feature in the book have also been changed.

My one hope for this book is that it acts as a catalyst for readers to go out and make their own discoveries of places on this island whose pleasures can never be exhausted. Everyone who knows Crete has their own favourite places they love to visit. That there is a healthy level of disagreement in such matters says much about the extent of the diversions the island has to offer.

I would like to express a debt of gratitude to my editor Jen Barclay – I am fortunate to have such a talented author to scrub up my manuscripts; Cheryl Perez who again has delivered the design and format for both print and eBook versions; my good friend David Richardson for another striking cover design; to all the readers who take time to write reviews; and my family, Denise, James and Lucy, Rebecca, Pete and Esther.

More Hidden Crete – A Notebook

As I blink awake, sun seeps through the slats of the shutters, seeking out shadowy corners of the room, bathing them in a light full of promise. It is a special time. That moment whenever I awake and realise I am back on Crete. That first morning when the sun slips a note beneath my door, pledging to shine brightly. Getting ready quietly, I ease out of the villa.

The sprinklers have started their early morning stint watering the gardens, and the flagstones that lead to the water's edge are still cool. Blooms in flowerpots and majestic pithoi perk up with their morning drink and glisten in the first flush of the new day. The cicadas are as yet silent, still sleeping in the trees which spread shade on the blossoms flourishing beneath. Cadmium scarlet, ultramarine, viridian, sienna, ochres, umbers and titaniums lustre, as if on a canvas painted by some celestial artist working from the richest of palettes.

Passing through a gate in the stone wall separating the garden from a dirt road that runs along its perimeter, I walk out along the small jetty. Bending down to break the surface of the water with my fingers, I nod in acknowledgement that it is unsurprisingly warm.

No wind ruffles the Gulf of Korfos as I stroll towards the village to buy bits and bobs for breakfast. A lone goat bleats plaintively in its scrubby enclosure by the bridge which crosses the narrow canal linking the gulf with the bay of Mirabello. A waiter from Kanali, just arriving for work, remembers me from last night when we ate in his taverna and stops for a chat.

Kanali is right on our doorstep here, and serves some of the best food to be had on Crete. Arriving at our villa well after dusk had settled, we were nevertheless not too tired to tuck into a shared meal of salt-baked sea bass, sardines and mussels, followed by kataifi oozing with lemon and cinnamon syrup. As well as a carafe of house white wine, I fear we may have drunk more raki than was judicious. The memory of this surprises me as I feel so buoyant this morning.

Promising to return to Kanali soon, I resume my walk across the cobbled bridge, past the lost city of Olous, which languishes submerged beneath the waters just offshore. On the beach are the dilapidated remains of a warehouse used to store the precious produce gleaned from the Venetian salt pans that lay on the other side of the road.

Even at this early hour it is hard to count how many times I stop to talk with friends old and new. It is an ideal way to readjust the pace of life to Cretan time; to reconcile myself again to one of the reasons I love Crete so much.

As well as researching my next book, we are in Elounda to see if we can find a small house to buy so we can return here more often. I lived in Heraklion in the 1980s, working as an English teacher. As an aspiring writer, I reluctantly left Crete to pursue a career back in England. Finding ourselves in a position now to purchase a house here and having the time to enjoy it, and as the majority of my writing now takes the form of books about Greece, to find a place near here would be ideal.

As if there were any need to, the bay could not be selling itself better. Like a sheet of polished glass, it brings to mind what catching sight of this secluded gulf must have been like for those early pioneers of air travel who took the flying boats of Imperial Airways from England, bound for Egypt or India. Elounda was a refueling station for the four-engined Short Kent biplanes which revolutionised passenger travel and mail services between 1928 and 1939.

The airline converted a 300-ton fishing vessel, which it renamed *MV Imperia* and moored in the bay, to act as a luxurious air terminal for passengers and crew making the stop on Crete. It is widely held that Winston Churchill broke a journey here to hold a secret meeting with Mahatma Gandhi.

The early days of passenger air travel were not without risk, and on the 22 August 1936 the flying boat Scipio crashed whilst attempting a landing in poor conditions in the bay. Two of the eleven aboard sadly lost their lives, the survivors rescued by the crew of the *Imperia*. With the outbreak of the Second World War, Imperial Airways stopped their operations in Crete and the *Imperia* sailed from the island when the Germans invaded in 1941.

By the time I return from the village with bread, honey, yoghurt, eggs and fruit the sun is making its presence felt. High in the sky now, its effulgence turns the sea a cobalt hue and bleaches colour from the village of Elounda across the bay. The first caiques have begun their workaday procession to and from Spinalonga and the beach beside the causeway starts to fill with sunbathers.

Today we will do little more than rest, eat and drink - a swim maybe before dinner at the wonderful and understated Anemomylos Taverna the other side of the square. I will start my journey to discover *More Hidden Crete* tomorrow, or maybe the next day…

Good Times for Plaka

The fortunes of Plaka on the north-east coast of Crete have blown hot and cold in recent times. With all the twists and turns in its blustery past, the fate of this small village has, for the most part, been linked to the island that lies just a ten-minute boat ride offshore. Spinalonga, or to give it its official Greek name Kalydon, has a sombre past, but now provides the brightest of futures for the villagers of Plaka.

Friends have owned a taverna here for many a year. Frequently I sit looking out over what is now one of the most iconic views on Crete, across the bay to Spinalonga. Sometimes I overhear visitors bemoaning how Plaka has changed. Indeed it has. Ask most locals and they will tell you that it has had a switch in fortunes for the better. The 'island of tears' is now bringing smiles to the faces of the villagers.

Spinalonga is now the second most popular attraction on the island of Crete after Knossos. Visitor numbers are edging up towards the half million every year. Many catch boats to the island from Agios Nikolaos or Elounda, but enough come to Plaka to make trade good, without the village being overrun. The tavernas lining the seafront do brisk trade in season and the shops dotted around see a steady footfall from visitors staying at the hotels and villas which have sprung up on the outskirts of the village.

Plaka sits at the end of the coast road going north from Agios Nikolaos. Here a mountain blocks the way to the Cape of Zefirion and the traveller is ushered inland on a pass which rises steeply to the villages of Loumas, Vrouchas and Skinias. Against this striking backdrop, the waters of the Gulf of Korfos lap a smooth-pebbled beach sheltered by the occasional tamarisk tree. The village is little more than the buildings which line this road and those on the seafront, where a short quay serves the needs of local fishing boats and the caiques that ferry tourists to Spinalonga.

Originally a tiny community, Plaka made a meagre living from the land and sea, taking olives, carobs and fish to market in Agios Nikolaos. When in 1903 Spinalonga was designated a leper colony, fortunes changed. Out of the misery of the patients compelled to spend their lives on the island sprang up a thriving economy built on servicing their needs. Upwards of thirty locals worked on Spinalonga and other villagers made a living supplying food and other essentials to the patients and staff. It was just as well, as the plight of the residents of the island had stigmatized the region, a perception that could so easily have destroyed their livelihoods.

The last patient left the island in 1957. Advances in medical science had made the colony redundant. The deserted island became a source of building materials for the mainland community and the colony's fabric fell into disrepair.

Following the downfall of the military dictatorship in 1974, it was the stirrings of tourism in Agios Nikolaos and Elounda which saw Spinalonga's potential recognized. By the early 1980s a few of the houses on the island had been restored and local fishermen had begun marketing boat trips to the former leper colony. The restoration remains a work in progress.

It is hard to go there and not get an eerie sense of the island's past. Getting off the boat, you walk through the entrance to the colony known as Dante's Gate. For lepers passing here, they knew it was unlikely that they would ever leave.

Through the gate, the colony looks not dissimilar to many a Cretan village. Despite the tragedy of the residents' situation I find it affirming to know they went about their lives, falling in love, marrying, having children, in a way that might seem unimaginable. There were shops, tavernas, a church and a hospital on the island. Standing on the main street surrounded by flowers in bloom, the buzzing of cicadas and cats basking in the sun, it is easy to get forget how tough life on the island undoubtedly was.

I can't remember how often I have visited Spinalonga, but it is apparent that one event changed the island from a popular tourist attraction to a must-see destination. In 2005, British novelist Victoria Hislop wrote a best-selling novel based on the leper colony and a family that had lived there. Her book, *The Island*, was later made into the popular Greek television series, *To Nisi*, which was filmed in and around the area.

Thanks to the raised profile of Spinalonga, it has received grants to continue its restoration. In summer the island is now lit at night. At sunset, after the last boat has departed and the island is left alone with its memories, there can be few greater pleasures than sitting in a taverna in Plaka contemplating Spinalonga's colourful past.

There is debate as to whether Spinalonga has always been an island. Some believe that the Venetians dug out the channel between what is now the island and the larger peninsula next to it. Whatever the truth of this, the Venetians certainly turned the island into a fortress in 1579 to defend the Gulf of Korfos from the constant threat of pirate raids and the growing ambitions of the Ottoman Empire. At the time there was no other way into the bay. The narrow canal to the south connecting the Gulf of Korfos to Mirabello was not constructed until 1898, when soldiers of the French Army stationed on the peninsula dug the channel.

The Venetians were responsible for constructing the walls that surround the island and the semi-circular fortress. They did their job well. Even after the rest of Crete was ceded to the Turks in 1646, Spinalonga remained impregnable. It was only given over to the Ottomans in a treaty signed in 1715 following a siege of the island. The Venetians also left another legacy, the island's familiar name of Spinalonga. This derives from the Greek 'stin Elounda', meaning 'to Elounda'. Unable to understand the language they adapted the words to 'Spina lunga' meaning 'long thorn' in Italian. This may account for the confusion over the island's name and why many Cretans used to prefer calling it Kalydon. Recently a pragmatic acceptance of the benefits the more familiar moniker can bring has led to its general usage.

Replete after a meal of marinated anchovies followed by a plate loaded with mixed fish in the Captain Nikolas Taverna we see our friends, the proprietors George and

Angelika, cross to our table brandishing raki and Metaxa.
We are in for a long evening, but who could complain. We
sit contentedly catching up with each others' news. Across
the pewter bay, the moon and starlight illuminate
crenellated walls and crumbling ramparts of an island that
has seen its fortunes change for the better, and with it those
of this exquisite village.

The Tree of Knowledge

One of the particular pleasures of travelling around Crete is discovering significant places which are off the beaten track. On doing so, I feel a sense of appropriation that only such experiences can incite. There is usually a story to even the smallest dot on the island's map; often there is more to such places than meets the eye.

I am sitting in the shade of an enormous plane tree which holds celebrity status in the tiny village of Krasi, hidden away just off the road from Stalis to Lassithi Plateau. Under this spectacular tree are laid out the tables and chairs of the local taverna; and I can think of few better places to while away my time. The tree is billed as the oldest and largest on the island. It is certainly impressive. So notable is it that a sign erected recently declares it a National Monument.

This gnarled platanus is believed to be 2,400 years old, meaning it started life almost at the same time Aristotle was born. Over the years the trunk has expanded to a girth of some 50 feet, supporting a canopy which spreads over the entire square. Two other plane trees that stand nearby are thought to be the progeny of this leviathan. Dwarfed by its grandeur they undoubtedly contribute to the appeal of this village which must be one of the most picturesque on Crete.

Across the road is a huge wall into which has been built a row of large, arched apertures, one enclosing a further two vaulted chambers. These structures hint at what is responsible for the immensity of the plane tree. Natural springs emanating from mountains around Lassithi find their way to the surface here. Making the land around the village extraordinarily fertile, throughout the centuries these springs have been harnessed to supply water to inhabitants of the village and the surrounding neighbourhood. The chambers are known as the 'Megali Vrisi' or the 'great fountain' of Krasi. Beneath one of the arches is a spring where locals can collect water and a trough where animals can drink.

Another vault houses a spout feeding a row of stone basins. These are public laundry rooms, originally built during the Roman period. Since then this has been a place where local women would congregate to do their washing.

The laundry rooms were restored in 1890. Like the square in which I am now sitting, the fountains were a focal point for village society. The springs which feed them were part of a water system that in Roman times supplied a 14-mile aqueduct stretching from south of the village all the way to the city of Lyttos on a site to the east of modern-day Kastelli.

The remains of this impressive feat of engineering are still visible at places along the course of its route, particularly in the area around nearby Tichos and Kastamonitsa. Tichos means 'wall', the name probably taken from the aqueduct which passed through there, remnants of which are in places 32 feet tall and more than 6 feet wide.

Although the aqueduct is now a ruin, the same springs still supply the village water, the happy gurgling of which provides a pleasant accompaniment to a carafe of wine. The abundance of water endows the village with a natural fertility, all around the green of walnut and silver of olive leaves flashing as they rustle in the slightest of breezes.

Inside the room supplying drinking water is an inscribed plaque depicting what looks like two cockerels on either side of a fountain. I am intrigued. With the aid of my dictionary I have a go at a loose translation of the words. I think it reads something like this: 'Thought, wisdom and beauty had a meeting a long time ago beneath the leaves of the plane tree in Krasi. Humanity, wealth, justice and liberty were all growing like the wild branches which sprouted those leaves.'

Above the plaque are three portraits that give a clue to the meaning of the inscription and to an important piece of village history. The pictures are of the Cretan author Nikos Kazantzakis and fellow intellectuals Nikos Veis and the poet Kostas Varnalis. On asking the owner of the taverna, I discover the tree is also known locally as 'Nikos Kazantzakis' tree'.

It seems that in the second decade of the 20th century the writer was a regular visitor here. Indeed, it was the family home of his first wife Galatia Alexiou. Another member of this illustrious literary group which would meet here to discuss the affairs of the world was the man who was to become Galatia's second husband, Marcos Avgeris.

Discovering this piques my interest. When I lived in Heraklion in 1982, the street my apartment was on was named Marcos Avgeris. I feel slightly ashamed that in all the time I lived there I never questioned who he was. It is only discovering that he was a member of the 'literary fellowship of Krasi' that has led me to look into his life.

Avgeris was a renowned doctor, poet, novelist and playwright and advocate of the political left for much of the 20th century until his death in 1973 at the age of 89. His wife Galatea was also a poet, writer and feminist. She was part of a literary dynasty which included her sister the novelist Elli and her brother the poet Lefteris Alexiou. Throughout her life Galatea would publish using her first husband's surname; she died tragically in 1962 following a car accident.

All the members of this literary fellowship were influential in shaping Greece's future and all led turbulent lives as the political pendulum swung left and right throughout the 20th century.

The village is remarkably coy about its relationship with these literary giants. For this we should probably remain grateful as the pervading air is one of a backwater not desirous of being discovered. For those keen to learn more about Kazantzakis and the fellowship there is a museum dedicated to him in the village of Myrtia where Kazantzakis lived as a child some 15 miles to the west of Krasi. Founded in 1983, the museum is well worth a visit. The building was completely renovated in 2009 and the exhibits are curated in such a way that for enthusiasts of the writer, his legacy is brought to life.

Here in Krasi, looking through the aperture beneath the plaque gives a glimpse into the bowels of this ancient aqueduct, which for so long has been a source of life to this out-of-the-way village. A local has set up a stall beside the spring to sell home-distilled raki, an entirely appropriate juxtaposition in this timeless spot; water and tsipouro, two drinks at the beating heart of Cretan life.

Kazantzakis' Tomb Revisited

Looking down over its rooftops Heraklion appears burgeoning, even in the crisis that has befallen Greece in the last decade. It is hard now to imagine the city of my first memories 35 years ago. How it has changed. But even then it had begun its transformation from the days when Nikos Kazantzakis called these streets home.

Arguably Crete's favourite son, the writer of *Zorba the Greek* among other classics of Greek literature died in Germany in 1957, and was buried here on the colossal ancient walls which surround the old town. This used to be a spot set adrift from the hustle and bustle of the dusty alleys and clamour of the capital. Now a tranquil island, its shores are washed by tides of new development as the city spreads forever outwards.

The terracotta roof tiles of traditional homes rub up alongside the dazzling white concrete of new apartments,

offices and shops. Dotted on the hillsides, emerald
swatches of well-watered lawns surround swimming pools
of luxury villas. All the while a glimpse of glinting sea
shines between the rooftops. To the south the hills stretch
away towards Knossos.

Criss-crossed steel trunks of cranes peep over the trees
that surround the patch of grass where a simple wooden
cross marks the author's grave, so poignantly engraved
with the epitaph 'I hope for nothing, I fear nothing, I am
free'. Few people visit this oasis of calm in an otherwise
restless town. The setting of this memorial remains fitting.
Always standing apart from the conformity of the
Orthodox Church, he was refused burial in consecrated
ground. Here he lies near the Chania Gate at the very heart
of the walls that were constructed to defend the citizens of
Crete's capital, by whom he is revered.

I decided to visit the grave on a wave of nostalgia which
has seen me unintentionally washed up in the city on my
latest visit to Crete to research this book. In what turns out to
be a pleasing act of symmetry, this journey began as did my
first in 1982. Then, as now, a strike forced me to take my
favoured method of transport to the island, the ferry.

Approaching the port at dawn brings back memories
of that first visit. A roseate glow emanates from the town
and the water burns a soft orange, gilded with a filigree of
silver. Memories reawakened, my desire to revisit the tomb

is rekindled. It is good to have been prompted to return to the place that celebrates the man so fundamental to my understanding of what it is to be Cretan.

Walking from the port uphill along 25 August Street towards Lion Square never diminishes that marvellous sense of anticipation. The road is now pedestrianised and the reduced danger of being run over makes getting a taste of the architecture a more relaxing experience than it once was. The church of St Titus, the Venetian Loggia and St Mark's Basilica are historical appetizers for the feast of delights the island has to offer.

Plateia Eleftheriou Venizelou, as Lion Square is officially known, is yawning itself awake, but I leave behind the sounds of waiters opening shutters and moving chairs, resisting the temptation to stop for coffee. The town's main market on 1866 Street is already alive with traders and early morning shoppers as I weave my way, emerging the other side of the eye of the town, climbing towards the imposing city walls.

Heraklion may have changed, but the tomb of Kazantzakis is a steadfast reminder of those elemental qualities which underpin the Greek character - a love of life, freedom and an intrinsic need to challenge authority. For this reason it is an ideal place to start my new journey, to reflect and retune to the Cretan way, which Kazantzakis so espoused.

Fire!

Dawn over the villa we have rented in Paleochora, the sun rising out of the sapphire sea bathes it in gold. The morning mist lingers low over the mountains inland. Amazed that I could share so much perfection with so few other people, I find it hard to wrest my gaze away and make the early start we have promised ourselves.

The aroma from the bakery also rises with the sun. We stop to pick up hot, crumbling pies not long from the oven, cheese (tyropita) and spinach (spanakopita). The smells of feta, dill and mint emanating from the warm bags becomes too much and we bite into the pies before even reaching Kandanos. Brushing crumbs from laps, we have the road much to ourselves save for a lorry collecting refuse and the occasional waiter returning home after a long night's work.

We are passing through Kandanos valley, skirting the western foothills of the Lefka Ori. This is fertile territory.

Having the highest rainfall on the island, the road between here and Floria passes through some of the most productive land in Crete. As far as the eye can see the landscape abounds with olive groves, vineyards and chestnut trees. The richness of the soil here has been valued for centuries and nearby excavations uncovered a mosaic floor which was dated as having been laid in the 3rd century AD.

It is believed that Kandanos takes its name from the ancient settlement of Kandanou which was destroyed by earthquake. The Romans, Venetians and Turkish occupiers all settled here. Byzantine churches dotted around the hills attest to the region's legacy but the absence of any ancient buildings in the village itself serves as a reminder of a violent history.

During the Second World War, in the first week of the battle of Crete, the invading German army was hell bent on securing Paleochora to stop the allies landing reinforcements or evacuating troops from there. Islanders from the surrounding area picked up whatever arms they could find and, despite being vastly outnumbered, held the German advance for some two days on 24 -25 May 1941.

Outraged by the resistance, the temporary commander of the island, General Kurt Student, ordered reprisals against the local population. With a brutality which was to become a German hallmark in their subsequent occupation of the island, troops were sent to slaughter the residents of the village and their livestock. Most of the buildings in Kandanos and the nearby villages of Kakopetro and Floria were razed to the ground and 180 people murdered. As a warning to others, signs were put up on the edge of the village. One read: 'Here stood Kandanos, destroyed in retribution for the murder of 25 German soldiers, never to be built again.' It now lies by the war memorial in the square, preserved for posterity when the village was rebuilt.

Today Kandanos is a peaceful spot. Tourists pass through on their way to the south coast, but rarely stop. Like many villages the population is in decline, with fewer than 400 residents. Kandanos has several tavernas and a kafeneo in the plateia. Already men are sitting outside taking their first coffee of the day as a woman in black mufti waters the potted geraniums surrounding the tables.

For those who take time to stop, there are numerous Byzantine churches which have been rebuilt since the war. Many contain damaged fragments of magnificent frescoes. To the south of the village is the chapel of Sotiras Christos, considered to be one of the most important churches on the island. Although its construction is relatively modern, inside it becomes clear that an older, original Byzantine basilica has been incorporated into a more recent shell.

Columns and decorated bricks are evidence of this inheritance as well as some faded 14th-century frescoes. It is widely held that this church was the seat of a bishop during the Byzantine period.

It is our intention to take a long circular route up to the north coast near Maleme, turning west to Kolimbari and Kastelli Kissamos then travelling south again skirting the rugged west coast before heading inland across the mountains back to Paleochora. So far the journey is familiar as it follows the road we use when going to Chania.

The sun is already hot and we stop at a periptero for cold drinks. These kiosks are usually found on street corners in every town and village in Greece, but this one appears to be miles from anywhere, perched in a layby on this country road. The name 'periptero' derives from the word for an ancient temple surrounded by columns. Today these small wooden boxes pay homage to the modern Greek gods of cigarettes and newspapers. With these two staple products now under threat, some believe the kiosks' days to be numbered, which would be a shame.

Kiosks were introduced to provide an income for war veterans and the coveted licences have been handed down through generations. Although they are regulated in size, fridges for drinks, freezers for ice creams and racks of newspapers and magazines spill onto the surrounding area. They are open all hours and I recall being able to use telephones in kiosks in Heraklion before the days of mobile phones.

The road twists and turns through other martyred villages as we head northward. Roadside traders are already at their stalls selling local honey, raki and olive oil. Just before Voukolies we catch a fleeting glimpse of sea through a gap in the hills before we start our decent and the road begins to straighten. As the land flattens we pass through orange groves and our route shadows the River Tavronitis towards Maleme.

It was at the estuary of this river that the Germans established a foothold during the battle of Crete by taking the nearby airfield. If you take the main road east toward Chania from the modern steel bridge crossing the river, you can see the remaining pontoon bridges used to cross the Tavronitis during the invasion.

Today we are going in the other direction and turn west along the coastal strip towards Kolimbari at the base of the Rodopou peninsula. This small seaside resort, just off the main road, makes a pleasant enough base for those wishing to explore unspoiled Rodopou. The terrain on the peninsula itself is severe and desolate and significant roads only penetrate as far as Afrata, Rodopos and Ravdouha.

Although a track of unpredictable quality does go further, I would not recommend it in anything but a four wheel drive vehicle.

The best way to see this isolated cape, still largely untainted by tourism, is either on foot or by boat. In midsummer walking here is uncomfortable as there is little shade; the best option is to go by boat from Kolimbari to Diktynna at the tip of the headland.

There has been a sanctuary standing on this secluded spot looking down on a sheltered, sandy bay since the 1st century BC. It is named after the Minoan goddess Diktynna, a daughter of Zeus, who was born in the mountains around the Samaria Gorge. In a story that resonates with that of Britomartis who inhabits the waters near Elounda, Diktynna was pursued by the randy King Minos and, in order to protect her virtue, flung herself from this headland. Rescued by fishermen in their nets, her rectitude was rewarded with immortality by the goddess Artemis. In gratitude to her rescuers, the goddess is said to appear at night to help sailors navigate the dangers of the coast. Further research has led me to discover that the legend is indeed the same as that of Britomartis with only the name of the goddess and the place of her demise being in dispute. Indeed in some dispassionate sources she is known as Diktynna/Britomartis.

The visible remains of the sanctuary to Diktynna are Roman, built during the rule of Hadrian in the 2nd century AD, and statues of both the goddess and emperor can be seen in the archaeological museum in Chania.

We have not time to explore the peninsula today if we are to complete our drive along the west coast, so reluctantly head towards Kastelli Kissamos. This is the furthest sizeable town west along Crete's north coast and has a harbour and a ferry port with links to the Peloponnese as well as the island of Gramvousa and Balos Bay. On first appearance, these might be the only reasons to stop at this utilitarian town which tips a wink to tourism whilst going about its day to day business of serving a thriving local community.

Driving through Kissamos is a nightmare as the road narrows and parking is chaotic. But the shops are good, and on the seafront the town shows a different face. Cradled in the arms of the Gramvousa and Rodopou peninsulas, the view is worth stopping for. There are plenty of places to take refreshment on the seafront, but Plateia Tzanakaki a bit inland seems to be the favoured spot for locals and savvy tourists alike. A town has stood here since Greco-Roman times and the recent addition of an archaeological museum in the former Venetian Governor's Palace is a revelation, housing magnificent Roman mosaics as well as a fine collection of Doric, Minoan and Venetian artifacts.

The port is a couple of miles to the west of the town. This is worth remembering if this is your destination, as it is a bit of a trek, particularly carrying luggage. We drive past the car park full of tourist coaches, a puffing, seagoing ferry in port impatient to sail, and turn inland. Leaving the north coast behind we head to Platanos, the last village of any size before we get back to Paleochora, some 30 miles southwards through the mountains.

Platanos is a considerable village which, however, doesn't see itself as a destination. This is primarily due to its proximity to the ancient ghost harbour of Phalasarna, which was lifted inland and 25 feet into the air by a cataclysmic earthquake in 365 AD. Since the remains of the harbour were discovered in 1859 by the British explorers Robert Pashley and Thomas Spratt, and the ongoing excavations that began in 1986, attention has shifted away from Platanos to the more popular tourist destination of the phantom port nearby.

Yet Platanos itself has its charms. The village has rooms for rent and good tavernas. Some of its population commutes to the nearby tourist spots for work, but most who live here make a livelihood growing olives and vegetables. It has its own oil mill as well as numerous shops, a bank and doctor's surgery. At the heart of the community is the village square, in which stands the imposing plane tree which lends its name to the village. The area is renowned for its sublime sunsets but it is barely lunchtime and we don't have time to linger if we are to complete our drive so make do with a brief stop for coffee in Motakis Café.

As we leave the village the view to the coast is sumptuous, the sea so blue its perfection is indefinable and the sun reflects like the finest of gold leaf off the greenhouses which lie on the narrow coastal plateau beside the bay of Livadi. Our way appears barred by severe mountains which engulf the coast. But this route is arresting and well worth any jeopardy it might entail. The increased numbers of roadside shrines make us aware that this switchback should be treated with respect. I try to simultaneously concentrate on the way ahead as well as taking in the breathtaking views. This is one of the least visited parts of Crete, its relative inaccessibility surely responsible for its unspoiled charms.

The road reaches a headland. From here the mountains skirt the coast and alarmingly drop away vertically at the crumbling edge of the tarmac. This is the bay of Sifnari and we stop at a roadside taverna next to a tiny 'super' market, both barely visible behind a dazzling display of climbing bougainvillea and potted geraniums.

An elderly woman sitting with her family gets up and greets us like long lost friends and leads us to seats on a small veranda under a canopy of vines. There is no menu, but we are grateful for a goat stew, the tender meat baked in lemon and orange juice with brandy, garlic and oregano and topped with grated hard cheese. We mop our plates clean with bread. I can see our host's disappointment that I will not sample the local wine, but I am conscious of the drive ahead and want to keep my wits about me.

A few miles on is Kambos. It is a beautiful enough village that also hides a secret of which few but the most enthusiastic walkers will be aware. Here is the head of the most westerly gorge in Greece and a well-marked but in places steep path wends its way beside the course of a stream to Platanakia beach some 1,000 feet below. In the village square there is a map outlining the route. I have not taken it myself but am assured it is worth the effort, although it is best to remember if you take the climb that you will need to hike back up the mountain!

Just after leaving Kambos our day takes a turn for the worse. Here the road narrows and gets more precarious as it makes its way to Kefali, frequently squeezing into a single track through local villages. Coming in the opposite direction are coaches returning from tours to Elafonisi, the turn off for which is in Kefali.

Out of nowhere I hear the screaming of a siren racing up behind. I squash the car as near the edge as I dare, letting a speeding fire engine squirm past. Rotors roar as a helicopter swoops overhead and round the next bend smoke billows from the tinder-dry mountainside.

There is nowhere to safely turn. Round a corner several cars have been brought to a halt at a road block set up by firefighters. Blazes like this pose a constant threat in Crete in the summer and can do untold damage, particularly in strong winds. In no time we have cars behind us and all the vehicles are trapped, unable to go backwards and with a raging fire somewhere ahead.

The traffic jam is substantial by the time police arrive. They erect another road block a mile or so back down the road at a place where cars can turn around. Car by car, coach by coach we reverse along the mountain road to a place we can do a tight three point turn and head back down the pass.

Unfortunately we get only so far. Now there is an impasse between traffic heading away from the fire and the cars stuck behind the road block still heading up the mountain, and it appears none of the vehicles can, or will, give way. Tempers are getting frayed. Drivers lean on their horns and get out of their cars to remonstrate. It is hot and the mood even hotter. After an hour stuck in this nightmare jam something suddenly gives and we gratefully inch down the mountainside.

Smoke still billows in the distance. It is unlikely the route will clear anytime soon. If we want to return to Paleochora we will have to retrace our steps.

Some hours later, tired and hungry we stumble into the Palm Tree Taverna. The blaze is talk of the town, and has now been put out. A hire car had caught fire trying to drive the dirt road from the beach at Elafonisi. Fortunately the driver and passengers had got away, but the blaze had soon taken hold of the surrounding countryside and it had required fire crews from both Chania and Kissamos, as well as the helicopter, to bring it under control.

We will try another day to explore the remaining part of our route. For now we gratefully settle for a snack of anchovies, fried zucchini and bruschetta with peppers and oil, accompanied by the most magnificent chilled Trebianno made by the monks in the monastery at Agia Triada. Outside the broad stretch of sand is deserted. The sea makes no sound on this most still of nights. In no time at all fatigue, food and drink take their toll and we take our leave and return to the villa on the beach.

Return to Elafonisi

In *Crete – A Notebook*, I wrote of a trip to 'Crete's Desert Island' of Elafonisi which I had taken out of season in the 1980s. I am aware that this is now a major tourist attraction. It is hard to avoid advertisements for excursions to this spot of great natural beauty. I include it here in the full knowledge that being so popular now, Elafonisi can hardly be described as 'hidden', but it does remain remote and out of season is still sublime in its desolation. As we are staying in Paleochora, we decide to take advantage of our proximity, and the daily ferry service, to take a visit. For anyone wanting to go to this now renowned beach, a trip by boat is without a doubt the best option.

If you are not close to Paleochora, a coach trip is an option worth considering. Many people do drive, but the roads approaching Elafonisi are not the best and in my opinion it is better to let another driver do all the hard work. There are also public buses which make the journey to the lagoon from Chania.

I had been on *Sophia B* before on a dolphin watching trip and it is good to know the vessel is still in commission. We seek out a seat under the shade of the coach house to starboard so we can watch the coast pass during the hour's voyage. The boat leaves at 10.00am and on this August day the heat is already nudging 30C. The breeze generated by our progress across a near flat sea is welcome as we clear the island just off the harbour at Paleochora and set a course parallel to the coast.

The boat is packed. Holidaymakers and locals alike join us in filling *Sophia B* to the gunwales. They too are armed with beach bags stuffed with towels, mats, snorkels, bats and balls, and carrying wind breaks and umbrellas. In my heart I already know that our destination will no longer be a haven of solitude.

That so much of Crete has remained unspoiled has always to me been something of a miracle. It is hardly surprising once the genie gets out of the bottle that such spots of natural beauty cannot be kept secret. It would be hypocritical to be censorious of such change, especially as the income from tourism is much needed, but part of me is nostalgic for the way things were.

Elafonisi is a small island connected to a sandy spur jutting out into the most turquoise of seas in the far south west of Crete. Visitors can wade across the sandbar in the tepid, shallow waters. The beach on the mainland is of the finest sand and has two faces, so whichever direction the wind is blowing the waters on one side are usually calm. Where the sea meets the land, brilliant white sand is tinged with hints of red and pink, the result of light shining off fragments of shells which have been eroded on the gently shelving shore for centuries. Small rocky bays and pools lie to the landward side and the occasional cedar tree affords a few much sought after spots of shade.

Sophia B confidently cruises west round Cape Krios where the mountains edge up to the coastline. Turning north out of the shelter of land a slight breeze ruffles the sea and streams the blue and white ensign of Greece astern.

We approach shore to the south of our island of destination, the captain navigating a maze of barely-submerged rocks to find landfall at a rickety quay a short climb round the cliffs from the main beach. It is only now that the crew announces the boat will return two hours later than usual to pick us up as they are attending a wedding back in Paleochora.

There are worse places to be trapped than in this Arcadian spot. The delayed departure will make it a long day in the sun, a fate more benign than that which befell a group of resistance fighters and their families during the Greek War of Independence in 1824 in a violent incident which turned this piece of paradise to purgatory. Hiding out on the island, awaiting rescue by ship from the Turkish soldiers who were hunting them down, some seven hundred men, women and children thought they had evaded their pursuers. Unable to track them, the Turks had set up camp on the beach. Unfortunately, one of the Ottoman army's horses escaped and waded across the sandbar to the island. In trying to recover their horse the Turks discovered the fugitives and attacked them. Most were slaughtered and any who did survive were sold into slavery.

We pick our way across rocks to a sandy car park by the beach which has become a temporary campsite for motorhomes from across Europe. Awnings, barbeques, tables and chairs are all set up in this impromptu village as we outsiders try to find a path across and make our way to the beach.

Leaving the car park the sands reveal themselves and it becomes apparent that even at this early hour there is hardly a spot to be had. Every sunbed and shade is taken. We set up base away from the main beach on a rock in the shade of a lone juniper tree beside a bay where several small boats bob at anchor. The warm sea proves a welcome relief from the scorching heat as we snorkel through crystal clear water over gently shelving sands and the occasional cluster of rocks. There are plenty of fish and starfish. I spot an octopus scuttling for the shelter of home across the seabed.

The mainland beach is served by a couple of cantinas and surf shacks catering for kite surfers and sailboarders. It may be busy, but the authorities have been careful to control and manage this valuable natural asset. The island of Elafonisi itself is a nature reserve. No sunbeds or umbrellas are allowed there. Not many tourists stray too far from their towels on the main beach, so for those who choose to cross the sandbar to the island itself, some sanctuary can be found.

The sea is calm on both sides of the headland. Some legends have it that the island was originally called Musagores. It was named after a temple dedicated to Apollo who, in one of his incarnations as the god of music, was known as Apollo Musagetes. This all-powerful deity commanded his constant companions, the Muses, to calm the stormy seas hereabouts with their music. Whether or not his presence is with us as we wade out to the island I don't know but the water is no deeper than knee height.

Leaving the noise of the bustling beach behind, the quiet hits us, along with the lemony aroma of false dittany, saltbushes and waxy smell of rock samphire. The status as nature reserve helps preserve the environment for many bird species which stop here on their migratory paths from North Africa and for the sea turtles who lay their eggs in the soft sand.

Paths wend between juniper trees, their wayward arms waving erratically towards the sea like castaways crying for help. The white trumpets of rare sea daffodils accompany the percussive rustling of the firmly-rooted marram grass on the fringes of exquisite beaches and coves.

At the western tip a lighthouse serves as a modern-day Muse to protect seafarers from these dangerous waters where in rough conditions any number of ships has come to grief. Still visible to divers, just offshore, lay the remains of the Austrian ship *SS Imperatrix* which ran aground in a storm in 1907 killing 39 people. A simple monument to their memory stands ashore.

Although it is not deserted, the prevailing sense on the island is one of solitude. We take advantage of the relative peace to swim and laze on the beach before strolling back across the sandbar to the madness of the main beach.

The delay in our boat's arrival has made it a long day in the exposed sunshine. We are grateful to see *Sophia B* rounding the headland of Cape Krios, shouldering her way towards the quay. I am pleased to have reacquainted myself with Elafonisi and will do so again but next time, not in August.

Imbros – A Gorge to Savour

Leaving my room in Chora Sfakion early, I pick up supplies from Niki's bakery and head for the bus stop at the square on the seafront. The waiter at Delfini Taverna is already watering his display of plants and shifting tables. He stops to chat and enquire why, through choice, I am up at such an hour. With a smile he unconvincingly complains about having to be up for work. I am catching the first bus out to Imbros to walk the gorge and am keen to do it in solitude and before the day gets too hot.

Although it is only May, in recent years the popularity of this walk has increased. Perhaps because it is less crowded, shorter and less challenging than the more famous Samaria Gorge 20 miles west, to which it runs parallel.

The bus driver hurls his coach round the switchback of bends as we climb the foothills of the Lefka Ori.

Although fear of driving this road has subsided with experience, its allure never ceases to take my breath away. And all the while behind us stretches the Libyan sea like a swatch of periwinkle silk, still languishing in the early morning haze.

The bus slows. We follow a goatherd in traditional dress, a crook resting across his broad shoulders, his dogs guiding the flock to pastures new. The clang, clink and jingling of bells cuts through the timeless quiescence of the landscape.

I alight at Imbros. The village from which the gorge takes its name stands on the southern edge of the Askifos Plateau, so called after a derivation the ancient Greek word for cup, 'skyphos'. The plain was at one time a large lake. Standing in the shadow of the imposing limestone peak of Mount Kastro that rears up 7,000 feet to the north west, all that I can see now used to be under water.

The bus stop is near the entrance to the gorge beside the Porofarago Taverna, serving simple Sfakiot food. I can't resist stopping for cheese pitta with honey and Greek coffee. I am the only customer, which bodes well for my walk if not for the hospitable brothers who own the business. They assure me that soon their tables will be full of hikers as those wishing to do the round trip of walking down and then back up the gorge (or return by taxi) frequently leave their cars in their car park. I want to start the walk before the sun reaches its zenith and the trek gets crowded. I say my farewells and head off.

The gorge begins 2,500 feet above sea level and descends towards the coast for 5 miles. At the kiosk I pay the entrance fee of 2 euros. The going here is easy with the gentlest of slopes leading to the edge of the plateau. Fig and almond trees flourish here with a sprinkling of holm oak and the ever-present cypresses. As the rough path narrows the walls gain height and slabs of stone reveal what is left of the ancient route between Chania and Chora Sfakion. It is easy to see how such a place would be ideal to mount an ambush, and many bloody battles were fought here during the Cretan wars of independence, notably in 1821 and 1867.

In the summer of 1941, it was along this route that a bedraggled army of 12,000 allied soldiers retreated. Defeated at the hands of the Germans in the Battle of Crete, exhausted they made their way to the south coast in the hope of being evacuated by ship to Egypt. Australian and Greek troops fought a brave rearguard action to delay the advancing German army and buy time for their comrades. Holed up in Chora Sfakion, those that made the coast hid from raids by German bombers by day. For three nights the soldiers were taken off the island in small boats ferrying them to British Royal Navy ships waiting offshore.

By the fourth night it was deemed too dangerous to make any more landings and those not fortunate enough to be rescued were left to their own devices. Remarkably, more than half the retreating army made their escape, while the rest were captured or disappeared into the mountains to join up with Greek resistance fighters. There is a memorial to the heroic actions of those who fought to save Crete on the seafront by the harbour in Chora Sfakion. The spot where a German plane plunged into the gorge during that battle is a reminder of its past as a theatre of war. Debris from the crash can be seen in the intriguing, chaotic war museum in Askifou, a few miles to the north.

The trees and mountains close in and the descent becomes steeper. The path changes from gravel to stone and the temperature noticeably drops in the shaded glades. I take a sweatshirt from my pack and pull it on as the exertion of the walk is not enough to combat the chilly air. This walk may not be as challenging as Samaria, but what it lacks in distance and difficulty it makes up for by providing solitude and time for contemplation.

Caves pockmark the grizzled visage of the rocks mottled white, grey and golden as the light casts shadows through the overhanging trees impossibly high above me.

Purple rock lettuce and white turban buttercups comfortably cling to the shattered stone faces with a confidence not unlike that of the goats which roam freely here.

I take time and linger. An ambitious hiker can walk the route in little more than two hours but I want to savour the experience. I have just reached the narrowest part of the gorge in that time. Known as Stenada, here the walls rise up 1,000 feet. Reaching out, my fingertips can touch both sides of the canyon. The striation in the rocks resembles a captivating abstract carving. The walls are cool to the touch. A disconcerting breeze squeezes past me. At times the path ahead is so narrow it appears as an entrance to a series of caves connected by a dank, dark passage.

The gorge opens at a stopping point by a hut beside an ancient Venetian cistern. The cabin is closed up, although I have been led to understand that in the summer water can be bought here. I would not trust this though, and always carry a good supply. Digging out my bag of goodies I bite into a spinach pie and guzzle some water.

Taking up the walk again, I pick my way across rocks brought down in a landslip, a reminder of the precarious nature of the terrain. The path narrows before revealing the limestone arch of Xepitira. Created by freeze-thaw erosion, this natural bridge looks like a flying buttress sketched by an ethereal architect to support the tilting wall of the canyon.

Passing through this gateway the gorge remains narrow, but something changes. The light reveals I am nearing the ocean, like Ariadne's thread leading me out of the labyrinth. A wooden sign announces there is 1km left to walk and almost immediately the Libyan Sea divulges itself in the distance.

The walk has taken four hours and I am ready for some refreshment. There are several restaurants in Komitades but I walk to the old village and settle down in a traditional taverna. Fragrant horta omelette, crispy salad, creamy, fresh mitzithra cheese and a cold beer revive the spirits and, refreshed, I decide to walk the 3 miles back to Chora Sfakion for a much-needed siesta.

Margarites –

Where Time Stands Still

The Venetian city of Rethymnon is the perfect base to explore the heart of Crete. If at any time you find yourself there, a trip to the potters' village of Margarites is unlikely to disappoint. About 20 miles from the city, in essence it is a place that has changed little over the years, providing a fascinating insight into a working Cretan village.

Taking the old road east towards Heraklion we pass under the new E75 near the village of Stavromenos on the coastal strip. From here the road rises quickly as it encroaches on the foothills of Mount Psiloritis. Continuing another 8 miles we turn right following signs to the village. Another right turn sees us on a track approaching Margarites, its brightly-coloured houses clinging as tightly to the edge of a ravine as its residents do to their traditional craft. Looking north the sea glints in the distance and the houses are ablaze with plants of every hue. Pots balance precariously on roofs, blooms drape from balconies and blossoming containers burst with colour at the roadside.

We park and head through the winding streets of the village, uphill to where most of the potteries are to be found. Peeping through open doors we see potters at work, some still using traditional treadle wheels while others use electric power. In courtyards everywhere their work is displayed, from unashamed tourist tat to huge traditional pithoi. These massive pots are now bought as decorative additions to tavernas, hotels and gardens, but originally were used to store oil, wine, olives and nuts and even as burial chambers. Fragments of similar vessels have been found dating back to Minoan times.

The largest of these pots stood taller than a person. Studies suggest they could hold over two tons of oil. Because of their size and weight, the base of the pithoi would be partially buried for stability and they could only be used on the ground floor of buildings. Surprisingly, these gargantuan pots were thrown on a simple wheel. The base was formed prior to coils of clay being added until the desired height was reached. The pot would then be turned and smoothed before curing in a clay oven fuelled by olive wood gathered from the surrounding hills.

Before the potters had trucks to transport their wares, they would travel from the village by donkey carrying tools, clay and even their kilns with them, in order to make pots for customers in situ.

If you come here in summer it is worth visiting the Margarites Pottery Collection. The exhibition is housed in a hall in the village and contains displays and information about the history of the craft on Crete, as well as explaining the process of making pots, from preparation of clay to firing, glazing and decorating.

There are more than twenty potters still working in this village. Many dig their own clay during the winter months from the plentiful deposits in the hills around. These days most of the craftsmen prefer the control of firing their pots in electric kilns, but some traditional stone ovens topped with brick domes stand like miniature temples in the yards of several studios.

I cannot help myself, I have to buy a piece of pottery when I visit. My cupboards are full of carefully chosen souvenirs of trips to Crete. Today I buy a smiling sun to mount on the wall in the garden; it is not the pithos I crave, but getting that home might be a challenge.

The beauty of Margarites is how little it has changed over the years. It may be smarter now and new technologies may have been introduced to make businesses more profitable, but the essence of this sparkling mountain village remains the same. It lives and breathes pottery. There is alchemy here in these magical hills, turning humble earth into works of art.

Before finding a taverna for lunch, we visit the 14th-century church of Agios Ioannis Theologos in the square. The portal to the chapel stands beneath a single-arched belfry with a cross at its apex. In the dusky interior the walls are decorated with faded frescoes, the most renowned a depiction of the nativity. It is hard to make out detail in the darkened paintings but when my untrained eyes adjust to the light, even I can see there is something splendid about them.

Soul satisfied, I am eager to feed my body. In a shady spot in the centre of the village we come upon a gem of a restaurant, with stunning views to match the authentic yet unforgettable food on offer. Sitting at a table in the welcoming Mantalos Taverna on a shaded veranda with views down the valley I order snails, rabbit stew and spicy sausages. As is often the case I give in to temptation and order far too much. The snails are served in a sauce of tomatoes, onions and parsley and the sausages have a deep smoky, vinegar flavour to which a carafe of house red wine is an excellent accompaniment. Slow cooked in the oven for hours, the rabbit in its unctuous spiced sauce just melts in the mouth.

Against the odds, I finish the meal and even struggle through the fruit and raki brought me by the manager, Costas. It is hard to leave this fine eatery, not just because I have had such a good meal but because I have eaten so much. I attempt to walk off my over-indulgence before realising I have forgotten my smiling sun. I needn't have worried. On my return to the tavern, Costas runs out waving a blue carrier bag containing my memento of an enchanting day.

Crete's Winter Wonderland

It is said that there is something special about the light in Crete. Even on the occasional leaden days of winter it exudes an expansive quality which is comforting. This morning is different. It is dawn and I awake to a prodigious white glow slipping through the shutters, painting the walls in zebra stripes. It stirs memories of childhood and excitedly I roll out of bed and slide back the shutter. Outside the world has turned white overnight.

On the mountains and high plateaux of Crete in winter, snow is a regular occurrence but on the coastal strip it is rare enough to be considered an event. My room is bitterly cold and I put on an extra T shirt under my jumper and am searching for another pair of socks when the phone rings.

George is as excited as I am by this unusual turn of events. He is hatching a plan to drive to Lassithi to take in the scene in all its splendour. Although it snows on Lassithi Plateau every winter, it is the challenge of driving the tortuous route in extreme conditions that appeals, and fortunately he has a Land Rover in which he assures me the heater works.

I have driven with George before both on and off road and have absolute faith in his driving skills. Won over by his enthusiasm, I agree to join him. I just have time to grab a coffee before I see the Land Rover confidently approaching along the road outside through virgin snow.

We decide to make our way to Lassithi via the road from Neapoli. My driver vigorously swings onto the main highway going west. There are a few vehicles feeling their way gingerly along the uncleared road and every now and then we pass a car that has been abandoned.

The blanket of snow that has covered the island has smothered all sound, the gossamer silence empyreal. The familiar village of Limnes is transformed, its church spires like decorations on a Christmas cake. Before we turn off the road I see the watchtower of the infamous prison in Neapoli silhouetted against the alabaster mountains and shiver at the plight of prisoners locked up there.

Neapoli used to be the capital of Lassithi prefecture before it was usurped by the young pretender Agios Nikolaos in 1904. The town still retains the air of past grandeur and its cobbled streets and impressive central square and cathedral recall the swagger of its former glories. In the snow the mien is one of muted excitement instead of the usual hubbub. We stop in the square and order hot chocolate from a streetside kafenio, staring through steamy windows at drivers gingerly navigating the road outside.

To the plateau from here is slow at the best of times, a good 20 miles uphill on tortuous roads which switchback into the mountains that enclose the sunken plain. But we have all day. The concentration George needs to coax his vehicle along this road preoccupies both of us and we are unaware of how long the journey is taking, and care even less. Few others have ventured out. We pass the occasional farmer on foot making his way to fields on the high terraces and see a couple of flatback trucks driving with a confidence only complete mastery of the conditions or extreme foolhardiness can engender.

I have happy memories of trips to Lassithi, although none in conditions like this. The first time I tried to visit, when roads, maps, and my own knowledge of the local landscape were not so good, the route petered out and the hire car ended up in a field somewhere near the top of a mountain. At that time the landscape was dominated by the extraordinary sight of thousands of windmills, their cloth sails glinting in the sun like a fleet of sailing ships.

After a hiatus of some years I returned to Lassithi, determined to show my children this unique scene. I remember well my disappointment on finding the windmills had all but disappeared, the only remaining ones being used for decorative purposes in taverna car parks.

Despite the demise of the windmills, the plateau is still unique. In summer it attracts many tourists, but in winter it can often be all but cut off by snow, although it is one of the rare upland plateaus on the island to be inhabited all year round.

The few roadside tavernas are all closed. In the snow they have become part of the panoramic vista which they usually gaze out upon. Along the route, perched on the side of mountains, boarded up kiosks still display signs hinting at their summer trade selling honey, raki, oil, wine and fruit.

We pass through the villages of Amigdali and Exo and Meso Potami before cresting the rim of mountains which surround the plain. What unfolds before us is other-worldly. From this height all we can see is a sea of dazzling white, as though a starched counterpane had been thrown over this mystical world 2,750 feet up in the sky.

For those who make their homes here, living in such conditions is worth the hardship. Although the windmills are no longer present, they have been replaced by electric turbines, thirstily sucking water, rich in alluvial goodness, to the surface. In the thaw the meltwater provides nourishment for crops that flourish here. In just a few months abundant fruit trees will be bursting with pink and white blossom above a carpet of wild flowers, and the earth bursting with first crop potatoes.

The plain stretches 4 miles north to south and 7 miles in an east-westerly direction. It is criss-crossed by paths which meander the green and brown patchwork of fields and drainage ditches. A road circumnavigates the plateau, connecting the small villages where locals make livings growing crops, rearing livestock, weaving or providing services to tourists.

We head for Tzermiado, the largest village on the plateau. George knows a restaurant he thinks might be open, even in this weather, and we are not disappointed. Stopping on the main road outside the taverna, its courtyard is clear of furniture and its pergola stripped of leaves. Through the misted up windows we can see lights and push our way in through the glass door. A smattering of locals is seated inside, escaping the Arctic conditions, warming themselves by the blazing, wood-burning stove and with glasses of raki. On learning we have driven from the coast, our host is intent on providing us with some of the fiery drink and offers to make a selection of mezedes.

Stuffed zucchini, dolmades, taramasalata, spinach pies, cheese - the food just keeps coming, all accompanied by a sweet red wine the like of which I have never tasted before but which is the perfect appetizer and accompaniment to the highlight of the meal: baklava served with mastika-flavoured ice cream. I have drunk mastika as a liqueur several times but have only had this flavour of ice cream once, in Lindos on Rhodes. To eat it with a honey drenched walnut and almond desert is pure heaven and makes every uneasy yard of our journey through the snow worthwhile.

The owner is keen to chat and I tell him how I miss the windmills. He laughingly recounts that they may be making a return, in the form of wind turbines. Farmers who had been persuaded to replace their wind-driven pumps with electric turbines in a drive towards efficiency have been lumbered with the ever-increasing utility bills. The irony of this is not lost on my host who tells me the farmers are seeking a European Community grant to fund the installation of the new turbines.

It is time to leave if we are going to get back to Agios Nikolaos in daylight. Bidding our welcoming host adios, we head back into the mountains. Looking down, the snow gives the scene a timeless feel, the only betrayal of human existence the smoke rising from the chimneys of villages on the edge of the plain. This might have been the view witnessed by early settlers as long ago as Neolithic times, since when this isolated spot has been almost constantly inhabited.

Since 6000 BC settlers have taken advantage of the bounty of this fertile land. The mountainous landscape was also ideal to conceal resistance fighters who throughout the centuries have fought to gain the island's freedom from numerous foreign occupiers.

It was the Venetians who sought to put an end to such threats. In 1293 AD they sent troops to burn down the villages and drive out the indigenous population who faced the death penalty if they returned. The whole area became known as the 'spina nel cuore' or 'thorn in the heart' of Venice, which tried to maintain its policy of depopulation for two centuries.

Eventually the ruling tyrants recognized that the lush lands could be used to their advantage. In the 15th century they allowed the area to be repopulated with Greek refugees escaping the advancing Ottoman forces in the Peloponnese. They even provided engineers to design and construct the irrigation and drainage system, the vestiges of which are still in use.

In some ways the journey back feels more precipitous, with the danger of skidding downhill, in my mind at least, ever present. But the experience is unforgettable, and I am grateful to be able to see one of my favourite faces of Crete displaying a different demeanor. Although I would not recommend the drive in winter, whether in spring, summer or autumn Lassithi Plateau still reveals a remarkable countenance that if possible should not be ignored. In summer the roads can get busy with coaches, but most are there to deliver their cargo of tourists to the Diktean Cave in Psychro. In the evenings the plateau is for the most part left uninvaded, and there are few things as agreeable as strolling on footpaths through the fields before having a meal in one of the numerous village tavernas.

As we head down the mountain towards Neapoli the road becomes clearer, the snow is melting and despite my reticence at taking the drive I am disappointed to see it go. The intense bleached light has given way to a plumbous, dusky grey, dampening the spirits as it wraps us in its chilly moist blanket.

A Walk Back in Time - Sougia

Sougia is hidden away on the south west coast of Crete, halfway between Paleochora and Agia Roumeli. It is 35 years since I have visited this enigmatic nook and I am concerned that the years might have taken their toll.

Much of Sougia's appeal lies in its inaccessibility; it remains a destination for those in the know. I first discovered it after walking the Agia Irini Gorge, which ends north of the village, a captivating hike still popular with those people aware of its existence.

Starting from the village of Agia Irini, I do not recall the walk being as easy as some have said. It is a challenging enough trek to foment a sense of achievement, but it is comfortable for healthy adults wearing reasonable footwear.

The canyon drops through the west of the White Mountains from a height of 1,800 feet over its leisurely 8 mile descent into Sougia. The final 3 miles of the walk is along a quiet mountain road. The gorge follows the course of a stream bubbling through shaded clumps of plane and pine trees. The well-marked path darts back and forth across bridges and, in spring, the display of wild flowers assaults senses already dizzy with the aromas of thyme and sage. The gorge is open all year, and unless there has been a lot of rain it is usually passable. In the summer months flowers give way to a riot of purple oleander bushes.

Like so much in Greece, these prolific shrubs come with a legend attached. It is believed that the name of the bush alludes to the ancient myth of Hero and Leander. These two young lovers were separated by the waters of the Hellespont, known today as the Dardanelles. The young man Leander's love for Hero, a priestess of the goddess Aphrodite, was so strong that every night he would swim the strait to be with his lover. She in turn would light a beacon to guide his way to her.

One stormy night the wind blew out the flame and Leander was buffeted this way and that by the raging waters. Fearing the worst, Hero called out 'Leander!' but the wind and waves were deaf to her pleas, and he was dashed on rocks and washed ashore, lifeless. When his lover found the body he was clutching a flower which she planted as a symbol of love. This was the oleander bush from which all others have flourished.

Ultimately Hero could not stand the pain of her lover's death and threw herself from the tower where she lived. Oleander bushes are poisonous to both animals and humans, and in many areas of Crete are used as natural fences to deter sheep and goats from straying too far on the hillsides.

At the end of the gorge the landscape opens up to reveal cultivated groves of olive trees running down to the coast at Sougia. The aptly named Oasis Taverna lies here, and the friendly owner is used to ordering taxis for walkers to pick up their cars. The alternatives are to walk into Sougia and get one of the infrequent buses to Chania, or catch a ferry to Paleochora, or east to Agia Roumeli or Chora Sfakion.

Staying in Paleochora, it is a great opportunity for us to see how Sougia has fared over the intervening years. We plan to walk there again. This time our trek will take us along a section of the E4 trail, returning home on the evening ferry which stops off at Sougia on its trip from Agia Roumeli.

We set off at daybreak as the walk is about 9 miles, and likely to take some time. Reaching the quay at Paleochora the waterside cafes are already in full swing, serving coffee and pastries to locals on their way to work. We are tempted, but the rising sun is a reminder that we want to make headway before it gets too high in the sky and slows progress. There is not a trace of a breeze. The sea is like polished glass. No ships are on the horizon, no boats have yet left harbour for Elafonisi or to ferry trippers to beaches along the coast. We make solitary figures traipsing past the town campsite until the well-marked path departs the road and follows the coast to the cluster of beaches known as Gialiskari. From here we climb away from the sea traversing the promontory of the cape of Flomes.

Looking back we can see Paleochora sparkling in the morning sun, its buildings like cubes of sugar scattered on the sea shore. Leaving the view behind we follow a wide dusty track. All around are the purple flowers of wild thyme, so crucial for the creation of honey sold by roadside traders throughout the island. I can't see any bees or beehives but the goats roaming here feed freely off the aromatic herb. The scent of thyme has pervaded these hills for all time. The ancient Greeks would harvest the herb to burn as incense, which they believed imbued their warriors with courage. It was the Romans who first recognized its culinary potential adding it to drinks and cheeses.

It is not much after 10.00am but the heat is starting to stoke up. Looking down we can see the bay of Lissos. There is no-one in sight. Here we are, standing above one of the harbours that used to service the ancient city of Elyros that reached prominence in the 3rd century BC. The city was sited near the modern day village of Rodovani, 8 miles inland.

Elyros, despite being the most important city in the region in the Classical Greek period and having been rediscovered by the 19th-century English classicist Robert Pashley, has yet to be excavated.

Lissos, however, revealed itself as a result of seismic activity. It was found again in 1957 when a goat-herd came across what was later discovered to be the largest collection of ancient statuary uncovered on Crete other than those dug out of the ruins of the Roman capital of Gortys. These statues are exhibited in the archaeological museums of Chania and Heraklion.

Walking towards Lissos, it becomes apparent that there are plenty of artifacts in situ to fire the imagination. All around, hidden behind rocks, trees and in undergrowth, is evidence of this ancient civilization. Broken, tumbled columns that once formed part of this important centre of commerce are a reminder of a city that flourished until as recently as the 9th century AD when the population fled in the face of Saracen invasion.

Subsequently damaged by earthquake, this bequest from the Hellenistic, Roman and Byzantine periods remains nothing short of extraordinary. Standing amongst the remains, alone with nothing but our imaginations, it does not take long to conjure up images of a thriving society of tens of thousands living in this bucolic haven. The town was important enough to have minted its own currency. Gold coins featuring the goddess Artemis on one side and a leaping dolphin on the other have been excavated from the site.

The most substantial surviving remains are of the Asklepion, a temple named after the Greek god of healing, which people would visit to be cured of ailments. The temple was built in the 3rd century BC next to a spring, the waters of which were held to have restorative powers. Although the statues found here have been removed from the site, there remains an outstanding mosaic floor. The half-hearted erection of a fence, now broken down, is all that stands between us and this incomparable piece of antiquity which was laid in the temple in the 1st century AD. From where we are standing, the far end of the floor has been destroyed but in the centre is a picture of a brown bird set against a vibrant blue sky, the outer edges decorated in geometric white and black shapes, circles, diamonds and squares. All about are relics of the town's former glories, scattered by seismic power across the hillside. Pillars, triglyphs, metopes, sima and granite blocks bearing Hellenic inscriptions are strewn randomly on the desolate dust and scrubland.

Near the temple are further reminders of the everyday lives of the former inhabitants. If the waters healed the sick, the nearby necropolis, believed to date from the Roman period, puts into perspective the mortality of all. Stepping up the hillside the tombs are like tiny stone houses with rectangular and arched doors huddled among olive trees, rustling a wispy elegy in the mountain breeze.

There are two Byzantine churches nearby, both utilising the remains of earlier building, scavenged from the site. The first is dedicated to Agios Kirikos, a saint murdered at the age of three alongside his mother Saint Julietta in Asia Minor during the persecutions of Christians by the Roman Emperor Diocletian. Kirikos is the youngest martyr celebrated in the Greek Orthodox Church. On the 14th July every year, the saint's feast day, villagers from Sougia scramble their way along the footpath or come by boat, to camp among the ruins of the ancient town. The following day they attend a service in memory of Kirikos followed by a celebratory festival.

Nearer the bay is a chapel dedicated to the Virgin Mary or Panagia. The sombre, slate grey exterior of the church is at odds with inside, which reveals several vibrant frescoes and a bright blue iconostasis. A closer look at the paintings divulges a chapter from their tumultuous history. The eyes of the saintly subjects have been scratched out, an act of vandalism believed to have been done by incumbent Muslim Turks during the Ottoman occupation.

The magical solitude and hidden treasures make it difficult to leave Lissos, but we would like to spend some time in Sougia before our evening ferry back to Paleochora. From here the trail rises steeply to an open clearing, where we take a last look at Lissos before dropping down into a bewitching gorge. Imposing walls throw a welcome shade as we pick our way through pine, carob and holm oak, oleander bushes, and the occasional rogue olive tree. In little more than an hour we emerge at the harbour of Sougia, which lies just to the west of our destination.

In the cliffs behind the port is evidence of a cataclysmic event that happened on Crete more than one-and-a-half millennia ago. In 365 AD a massive earthquake hit the region, driving a huge wedge of lava under the west of Crete, lifting it out of the sea. This is more clearly exemplified in the 'ghost harbour' of Phalasarna on the north-west coast, but here in the rocks above the quay the tidemark of the original sea level can still clearly be seen.

A long beach stretches to the headland way past Sougia. The occasional clusters of beach umbrellas barely make a mark on its wide expanse of pebbles. At nearly a mile in length the most extensive beach in the south west of Crete is all but deserted. It is hard to believe that this beautiful shoreline could ever get crowded, and I am assured that it is always possible to find private space here.

The ramshackle nature of the village is beautifully camouflaged by an abundance of flowers. Some believe Sougia to be the dwelling place of the Cyclops of Homer's *Odyssey*, others might describe it as a one-eyed place, but herein lies its enduring charm. I am not disappointed. Sougia remains unspoiled by the march of tourism. If anything, it has cleaned up its act a little since I was last here.

To the west is the small church of Agios Panteleimon. White stone with a terracotta-tiled, arched roof, a covered terrace and stand-alone belfry surrounded by a graveyard, this church is unexceptional in all but an anecdote about how it was built. The story goes that a local saw a vision of a Byzantine chapel which had once stood in this place. The dream charged the villager with ensuring a new church rose on the same spot.

Further investigation duly found the remains of a church with a mosaic floor picturing geometric shapes, and vibrant-coloured birds and animals, similar to those found at the Asklepion we have just visited. The new church, dedicated to Saint Panteleimon (the all-compassionate) was built after the Second World War when Sougia was reestablishing itself as a village. The saint, one of the Holy Unmercenaries who healed the sick without taking payment, was a 4th-century martyr, murdered for his beliefs during the Diocletian prosecutions.

The plans for this new church, however, did not match the ambition of its Byzantine predecessor, a larger, three aisled building. Construction of the new chapel went ahead, on top of the priceless mosaic, and the unsympathetic design being smaller and of a different shape left the ancient floor protruding at the base of the new chapel. Sanity eventually prevailed and much of the mosaic was removed and put on display in the Archaeological Museum of Chania. Some pieces of the floor remain, evidence of its original footprint and a reminder of this wonderful eccentricity.

Sougia, now a soporific village, was once a town of no little significance from Hellenic times right up until the early Byzantine period. The name is a derivation of Syia, from the word for 'hog' (sys), after the pigs that used to run wild, scavenging red acorns from the forests of holm oak which surrounded the town. At the eastern end of the modern village the beach is known as the 'bay of pigs', allegedly a derogatory term used by some locals who disapprove of the nudism which is practiced there. I prefer to think it is a reference to the origin of the village name, which has been long forgotten.

What is known is that Sougia, like neighbouring Lissos, used to be a port for the city of Elyros. In 300 BC Sougia got together with that city and Lissos, to join with other powerful towns in south-west Crete, Yrtakina, Tarra and

Poikilassos to form the Confederation of Oreians. This alliance was so powerful that in time it was joined by the Carthaginians. Sougia's prosperity was built on trading and fishing and it flourished for well over a thousand years until marauding Saracens from North Africa laid waste to the town in the 9th century AD.

Its remote location meant that Sougia was to remain a backwater for the next thousand years, the destination of wandering goatherds and itinerant fishermen. Following the Second World War the village was established as a stop off for ferries from mainland Greece, trading and delivering goods to help rebuild the stricken economy. These were carried by donkey inland across mountain trails as there were no roads. When the road was built linking a newly revitalised Sougia to the north of the island the village looked destined to sink once more into sleepy obscurity. Had it not been for the 'discovery' of the spot by hippies in the early 1960s it might have remained that way. Unlike those who formed the famous commune in Matala 60 miles to the east, their secret was more closely guarded, but through word of mouth the delights of Sougia were whispered and slowly it became a small but established micro resort.

'Slowly' is very much the byword here, both in terms of development and pace of life. Fortunately locals realise that Sougia's face is its fortune and developments that might spoil its appeal would be counterproductive. Since I was here last there are a few more rooms to rent, the paintwork brighter and floral displays even more vibrant. There are no banks or, at the moment, even a cash machine.

Plenty of excellent tavernas line the wide beach, which runs down to the Libyan Sea. Quite simply, this is Sougia's appeal. A place you can escape the day-to-day cares of life in a blissful cycle of swimming, sleeping, reading, eating and drinking. Who could want for more? After our walk we are in need of food and sit down to a feast of barbecue-grilled sardines with Greek salad and cold beer in frosted glasses.

A swim and an afternoon nap are the order of the day as we await the evening ferry to Paleochora. Our vessel squarely elbowing its way towards us in the distance is our signal to pack our bags and head for the quay. The small car ferry *Samaria* is on duty today, carrying its cargo of walkers from the base of the Samaria Gorge at Agia Roumeli. We arrive several minutes before our ship, the vessel a splendid triumph of functionality over beauty as though constructed out of a child's blue and white Meccano set.

Not to waste time the skipper navigates to feet from the quay, the ramp is dropped and, as no vehicles are embarking, the captain dispenses with the need to moor his ship which is kept on station using engines alone. Within minutes *Samaria* is reversing before thrusting forwards in a gentle arc westwards. We find a seat at the rail on the upper deck among the backpacks, poles and other paraphernalia of sleepy hikers.

A full moon is already in the sky, as though gatecrashing the titian splendour of the sun's party, arriving to chase it over the horizon. It is a short 40 minute sail home along the coast where *Samaria* concludes her day's work.

Picking up our car we head along the coast to Grameno, where we are welcomed at the taverna which shares its name with the village. The food here is as authentic as it gets and it is a great place to indulge in Cretan specialities. They do wonderful mixed mezedes. Tonight we are indulged with tender, sweet cockerel in red wine, pork in orange sauce, lamb baked with potatoes redolent with mountain herbs, goat cooked with bitter horta harvested from the surrounding hills, rabbit and creamy mizithra cheese, goat and wild almonds and beetroot and onions. The poverty of the origins of these dishes is certainly at odds with the delightful richness of their flavours. The red wine is so deep it is almost brown in hue and with a strength and flavour to match. A generous plate of fruit and endless raki follow and we decide to leave the car here until morning and stroll the mile or so back home.

A Boat to Balos

Somehow, until now, I have managed to avoid visiting Balos beach on Crete's north-west peninsula and the twin islands of Gramvousa that sit just offshore. Put off by reports of the condition of the road to Balos or boats brimming with sightseers, I had yet to put in place plans to visit these remote spots in a way that I could best appreciate their solitary beauty. Mentioning this to a friend he gave me details of a skipper who had a caique in Kissamos who would organise a trip, and we might catch some fish as well. He was right.

We leave Chania with an autumn dawn, the moon giving way to an early sun impatient to assert itself on a day which is already showing its sparkling intentions. Beneath the morning mist the sea is being polished, transformed from galenite to shimmering silver.

The city traffic is light as we head west along the coast through its straggling resort suburbs, early-rising shop owners putting out their pavement displays and bar owners clearing the detritus of the night before. An occasional group of tourists stands anxiously, staring in hope that they are in the right place for today's excursion pick up, as women in black weeds lug supplies of newly-baked bread.

The mist burns off, revealing the secluded isle of Agia Theodori coming awake offshore. These days this solitary spot lies uninhabited all but for the kri-kri goats that make it home, one of only several places on Crete where these endangered endemic ibex find sanctuary. They are fiercely protected.

The goats became nearly extinct in the years following the Second World War, during which they were a valuable source of food for the starving population. Since then progress has been made and numbers of this emblematic creature have increased more than ten-fold, but they remain under threat from hunters, disease and hybridisation.

Kri-kri are notoriously shy creatures whose agility lets them escape the gaze of all but the most determined as they can leap from the most precipitous crags and cling to the side of all but vertical mountainsides. I have laid eyes on them only once before, while walking the Samaria Gorge, which was in part established as a national park for their conservation. They are important to Cretans, as through kri-kri can be traced a line going all the way back to their Minoan heritage.

With their long-curved horns, these beasts are clearly discernible on fragments of frescoes and pieces of jewellery uncovered by archaeologists. From this distance nothing can be seen of the recalcitrant creatures but it is reassuring to know that they are being protected on this sanctuary.

They are in good hands. Legend has it that the island and its smaller acolyte, Mikros Agios Theodorus (hidden from view to the north), were at one time a fearsome sea monster. Approached from the sea a giant cave gapes like the hungry jaws of a behemoth set on devouring all in its path. To save Crete, the gods intervened, and just in the nick of time turned the islands to stone. In 1583 the ruling Venetians commandeered the petrified monster as a fortress to protect Crete from attack by marauding pirates and later the acquisitive intentions of the Ottoman Empire.

Along the coast tourist developments segue until Platinias, after which holiday apartments flourish alongside clumps of reeds, olive, lemon and orange groves. We are approaching Maleme, the site of one of the most pivotal episodes in the history of modern Crete.

Just through the village lies an airfield; now a base for the Greek Air Force this was the focal point of the Battle of

Crete in 1941. Overlooking the aerodrome is a piece of high ground, named by the allied forces as Hill 107. Determined to secure the strategically crucial island of Crete, on 20th May that year the Germans launched the largest airborne assault that had ever been attempted. To get a foothold on the island, paratroopers mounted an attack on Maleme. Despite heavy German losses, a breakdown in communications led to the New Zealand troops who held Hill 107 withdrawing, allowing the invading army to capture the airfield, and land reinforcements and supplies.

From that moment allied troops were in retreat. Fighting a rearguard action, they withdrew across the mountains to the south of the island, where many were evacuated by ships of the Royal Navy. At the bottom of Hill 107 looking out to sea is the beautifully tended German War Cemetery, where the bodies of 4,465 invading troops have been laid to rest.

An uphill walk from the village of Maleme itself, this cemetery is a poignant memorial to the German soldiers who died during the invasion. With an extraordinary generous spirit of reconciliation the Greek government granted permission for the graveyard, which is maintained under the auspices of the German Graves Commission.

Rows of granite tablets lie on the ground marking the double graves of fallen soldiers. Between these simple stones grows a carpet of blood red marigolds, their golden hearts warmed by the sun which relentlessly beats down on this site overlooking the sapphire sound of distant Chania. The graveyard sits against a backdrop of the towering White Mountains to the south, the Tavronitis riverbed winds seawards to the west and to the east, on a clear day, can be seen the Monastery of Gonia far away in Rethymnon. The symbolism of this spot is intended to bring to mind the four main theatres of war on the island, Maleme, Chania, Rethymnon and Heraklion.

From 1974 until his retirement, the cemetry's caretaker was George Psychoundakis, a hero of the Cretan resistance and author of *The Cretan Runner*. Born into poverty, the young shepherd had acted as a dispatch runner for the SOE (Special Operations Executive) under the command of Patrick Leigh Fermor, often operating in the most extreme danger behind enemy lines. Leigh Fermor translated Psychoundakis' book into English and it was published in 1955.

Our skipper Spyros is already busying himself aboard his vessel as we arrive at the quay. A sturdy, classic caique of some 40 feet, its reassuring, well-maintained white hull is trimmed in red with teak decks and varnished superstructure. We are welcomed aboard, the engines already chugging in preparation for departure. With Spyros at the helm the crewman Ilias casts us off with a nonchalance born of experience. He manages to perform this manoeuvre without the inch of ash which balances precariously from the cigarette wedged in his mouth falling into the sea.

Once adrift our skipper sets a course seaward, his boat easily sliding over the slightest of swells. There is little wind, any there might have been held at bay by the giant arms of the capes of Spatha to starboard and our heading of Vouxa. The wash from a ferry to Kythira way to the north barely registers as we cut through the clear new day, drinking coffee at the guard rail, the occasional spittle of spray a rare reminder of our progress. Astern our wake is the only tie we have to shore, unravelling as we head seawards.

It is times such as these that Crete generously engenders. Living in the moment is the only concern, not thinking of our destination or looking to shore. Full to the brim with contentment there is no room for the most fleeting rogue worry. Our pace of life is determined purely by the motion of our craft through this endless sea. Looking downwards the boat rises and falls to the rhythm of its own bow wave, all thoughts of home ports or new horizons forgotten.

None of us is in a hurry to break the spell by fishing, to Ilias' incredulity. He baits up trolling lines, playing out the hooks from the cockpit as we sit entranced, enjoying this spellbinding moment. A silver, flitting fish breaks the surface, casting a fleeting rainbow. Excited, Ilias shouts to his skipper to slow the engines so he can heave in the lines. Only two fish have succumbed to the lures. Undaunted our crewman rebaits the hooks and throws them astern.

The next hour is punctuated by the hurling and hauling of lines as we stop start our way across the gulf of Kissamos. Buckets slowly fill with silver sardines as a triumphant Ilias appears to grow in stature with every fish he catches.

Spyros signals to his mate to bring in the lines as he pilots closer to the rocky shore. A huge cave is described by the captain as the site of an ancient shipyard called Tarsanas. I have since tried to find out more information as to the authenticity and date of this but can find no mention of the cave other than what our skipper told us.

We are close to the ancient Roman town of Agnion at Cape Korykon, where lie the remains of a temple to the god Apollo. In the absence of evidence to the contrary I envision this to be the place where the ruling Romans built their galleys. Agnion was the Roman outpost at the far north west of the island, many days' march away from their capital of Gortys in the south.

In the 1st century BC pirates operating out of the rocky coves of Crete had become a serious threat to the Roman Empire, intercepting shipments of grain en route from Africa to the capital. The pirates outnumbered and outsmarted the

Roman fleet for decades until their existence was seen to pose a deadly threat to the future of the Empire.

By 67 BC the Romans had had enough. They charged the commander Pompey the Great with the task of quashing the pirate threat. With ruthless haste, within three months this brilliant military tactician had cleared the seas of the mercenaries who ceded power to Pompey. The role of the Roman navy then became one of policing the coast and Cape Vouxa played a vital role in their defensive strategy. Was it from this very cave that the lightweight biremes, powered by 25 pairs of oars, were launched to patrol the eastern Mediterranean?

Along the coastline is evidence of a more verifiable phenomenon. The clearly visible markings of sea erosion on the cliffs show how the western end of the island is rising out of the sea. Crete lies above the juncture of the Earth's African and Eurasian tectonic plates, the friction in this unstable relationship causing lava to flow through the fissure forcing the coast upwards. The constant nagging of the two continents is usually gradual but, as mentioned before, in 365 AD an earthquake drove basalt under this end of the island, raising it into the air, leaving the former shoreline high and dry.

There is little time to ponder this event and the devastation which must have been caused by the resultant tsunami. We are anxious to stay ahead of the cruise boats to Balos, which will be following in our wake. Approaching Cape Vouxa a slight breeze ruffles the surface of the sea, pitching the bow of our vessel as she turns her face towards the passage between Crete and Agria Gramvousa.

Its name couldn't be more apt. Meaning 'wild' Gramvousa, this rugged, uninhabited island is the far north-western tip of Crete. There is little sign of the hand of man here, except for a lighthouse warning shipping of the many unexpected dangers this coast holds. We pass on the inshore passage of the wild island, the last landform of any significance before the island of Kythira just off the Peloponnesian coast of mainland Greece.

As we round the cape and the boat changes heading to the south, along the island's west coast, ahead lays Imeri Gramvousa like a petrified oil tanker moored offshore. 'Imeri' means 'mild' Gramvousa, which from afar might not seem the most accurate word to describe this desolate rock. The wreck of a ship lying aground and rusting between two bays to the south of the island is testament to the dangers of these waters and further questions the island's benevolent epithet.

The rusting hulk is all that is left of the cargo ship *Dimitrios P* which set sail from mainland Greece in the last days of 1967, on course for North Africa. Running from a severe storm, the captain sought shelter to the south of the island and in a last ditch attempt to save his ship let go two anchors in the bay. In the force of the storm, one anchor chain snapped and the other could not hold the fully-laden vessel. In raging seas, his engines were not enough to pull him away from shore and the ship ran aground. The crew escaped ashore to be rescued two days later, but the wreck remains, a gruesome reminder of the perils hereabouts.

Our plan is to visit the beach at Balos first and then return to Imeri Gramvousa later, keeping one step ahead of the tour boats. It is hardly surprising that this picture-perfect lagoon is popular. Along with the palm forest at Vai and Elafonisi island, it is one of the most celebrated beaches on Crete. Getting here early, it is easy to see why. Balos is difficult to access by land, although some 4x4 tours do head this way, so out of season or either side of the middle of the day this much vaunted paradise remains just that.

We drop anchor. It holds firm in the surprisingly muddy sea bed which shelves down from the white sand beach around a lagoon that stretches from the Gramvousa peninsula to the Cape of Tigani. Facing onshore, behind us lies the basking Imeri Gramvousa and inland the imposing Platiskinos range topped by Mount Geroskinos in the distance.

Glinting pink specks peek through the ivory sand hinting at the secrets of the forging of this beach. Thousands of years of grinding, sanding and smoothing shells into pearly grains have created this, an Eden washed by waters striated with azure, turquoise, cobalt and any other shade of blue yet to be invented.

Wispy grasses and half-buried boulders inhabit the hinterland of the beaches. The inevitable umbrellas and a cantina give notice of the oncoming onslaught on forthcoming boats.

Scrabbling across rocks on the south side of the lagoon we make our way along the Tigani peninsula. In Greek tigani means 'frying pan'; whether this spur of land is so named because of its shape or the prevailing temperature I don't know, although either would be appropriate.

There is a small dilapidated chapel dedicated to St George here and a cave where a plaque commemorates its grizzly past. Like many other places of sublime beauty on Crete this one is tainted with a bloody history. It was in this cavern that women and children seeking refuge from the occupying Ottomans were put to the sword by Turkish troops in 1825.

A pair of predatory falcons hovers and swoops. On the horizon the clearest blue sky melts into the sea with only the faintest hint of change in its elemental being. This whole area, both land and sea is protected for flora and fauna alike. Seals, turtles and dolphins are frequently spotted in the shallow waters, and cormorants nest in the caves on the cape. Looking back from the hill on the promontory it is easy to see why this beach holds such a reputation. The panoramic view is close to perfection.

Out to sea, the telltale sign of a growing mote of white forging forwards is a reminder that it is time to move on. Heading back aboard our caique we weigh anchor, making Imeri Gramvousa by the time the ship carrying upwards of 1,000 passengers passes inshore.

There are two small bays at the south of the island, between which the wreck of the *Dimitrios P* lies stricken, its back broken, rusting in the shallows. Spyros steers a course for the westerly cove where we moor at a quay. A path leads to a white sandy beach, which lies at the foot of an imposing cliff; high above stands a huge redoubt, constructed by the Venetians during their tenure here. From a lofty 450 feet above the sea, the walls which guard the fortress form a triangle. It took a team of master craftsmen five years to build, the final masons completing their work in 1584.

The fort held this strategic position to defend the north-western boundaries of Crete. Under Venetian command it was home to 3,000 troops. The defences were so impregnable that, even after the island fell to Ottoman forces in 1669, Imeri Gramvousa remained in Venetian hands along with the two forts at Souda and Spinalonga.

Venice's power was built on trade and the protection these castles provided for their shipping routes invaluable. In the end it was not force which delivered the island into Turkish hands but an act of supreme treachery.

During La Guerra di Morea (Morean War), the sixth conflict between the Venetian Republic and the Ottoman Empire, the commander of the island, Luca della Rocca, succumbed to bribery and surrendered Imeri Gramvousa to the Turks in 1692 without a shot being fired. He retired to live out his life in some luxury in Constantinople.

Realising the strategic importance of the fortress, the Turks hauled more than 60 canon to its ramparts. The island remained in Ottoman hands until the Greek War of Independence. It was then that Cretan revolutionaries managed to wrest control of the fort, only to see it fall to the Turks again when the Greek Commissioner for the island, Emmanouil Tombazis, failed to see the threat posed by a force of 12,000 troops under Ottoman commander Hussein Bey, and succumbed in 1823.

Not taking defeat so lightly, two years later a band of 350 Cretan soldiers disguised themselves as Turks and stormed the castle. The rout complete, they hunkered down in the fort, their victory becoming a significant morale boost for the forces of Cretan independence. Soon a settlement was formed on the island with shops, a school, and a chapel dedicated to the wives of the invaders, who had taken to piracy (Panagia i Kleftrina).

Although the Turks were unable to regain the rock they were successful in blockading it. The siege led the desperate Cretans to increasingly rely on attacking passing ships to survive. Although able to keep body and soul together, their success was also their downfall. The pirates did not discriminate as to which ships they targeted and their wholesale plundering caused foreign powers to put pressure on the fledgling Greek government to put a stop to it.

So it was that in 1828 the Greeks themselves led a British and French fleet to besiege the island. Their superior force overcoming any resistance, custody of the island was handed to the British and subsequently back to the Turks under the revised London Protocol of 1830.

Wary of further assaults on the castle, the Ottomans drafted in reinforcements and shored up its defences. The island remained in their hands until governance was taken over by the 'Great Powers' of Britain, France, Italy and Russia in 1897.

Nowadays the only invaders are tourists. A well-trodden path from the quayside winds behind the beach up the rocky knoll to the castle, passing beneath the vaulted arched entrance through stone walls in places more than 50 feet tall. Nervously peering over the parapet, the views are spectacular. Looking north past Agria Gramvousa an endless blue stretches all the way to the horizon. The only thing breaking this wonderful monotony is the occasional ship plying its trade to Piraeus, Italy, Africa or the Middle East. To the south is the Bay of Balos and east the rugged rocks of the mainland peninsula. The limestone walls merge seamlessly with the sheer cliffs supporting them, creating what must have been a daunting obstacle to any who sought to invade here.

Inside the fortress are remains of the Church of the Annunciation, a gunpowder store, water tanks and a domed lookout post. From here we can already see the first sightseeing boats steaming towards the island from Balos.

We were intending to have a barbecue on the beach but Spyros has other plans. Already the engines are ticking over as we clamber aboard. He has a grill which can be bolted to the guard rail so we set off for a quieter spot. Finding the perfect anchorage back around the Vouxa headland in the shadows of Agnio, engines off, our vessel gently tugging at its grapple we tuck in to grilled, salty sardines, bread and salad and a bottle of aromatic Malvasia di Candia wine from the cool box. The wine is sweet but the chill tempers the taste. Spyros wants us to try it as he tells us the grape variety goes back to the days when the Venetians built the fort on Imeri Gramvousa. Drifting here in the Gulf of Kissamos with not another vessel in sight it is easy to ponder how little here has changed since that time.

Donkey Island?

From a distance the island looks flat. Like a white plate laid gently down on a tablecloth of blue. We are on what must be one of the first tours to Chrissi this season. Our ship, *Aristovoulos,* is less than quarter capacity, the reassuring thud of the engines confidently assaulting the peaceful morning. No doubt the Minoan traders who sailed these waters 5,000 years ago would have settled for that noisy reassurance as they navigated their precarious craft to and from the mainland across this same 8 mile stretch of unpredictable Libyan Sea.

Nowadays this isolated island is for the most part uninhabited, although three conservationists have temporary residence there. During the Minoan period Chrissi was a thriving centre for stock rearing and fishing. Its most valuable exports, however, were dyes made from shells, produced to colour the purple and red robes worn by the dynastic kings of Crete

A few miles west of our port of departure, Ierapetra, stood the Minoan settlements of Fournou Korifi and Myrtos Pyrgos. It was from somewhere near what is now the sleepy village of Myrtos that the Minoans set sail. This would have been a venture rife with jeopardy. Wall paintings discovered on Santorini depicting early Minoan craft show them to be small vessels hewn out of pine, and sailed by a crew of only a few men. These were not the warships of the same period powered by oarsmen but sleek trading boats, aboard which sailors must have felt vulnerable to the fierce meltemi winds which regularly blow in from the west.

Today the journey from Ierapetra is less than an hour long and the sea has been kind to us. Even from afar it is easy to see why this island has been designated an area of outstanding natural beauty. As such Chrissi is the most southerly spot in Europe to be protected under the Natura 2000 scheme. The ecological importance of the island has been recognised mostly due to its forest of Lebanon cedars, the largest remaining in Europe. The trees cover almost a quarter of this low-lying piece of rock which was forced up out of the ocean by a tumultuous undersea volcanic eruption millions of years ago.

The waters surrounding Chrissi are shallow, at their deepest no more than 70 feet, for an area covering six times that of the island. The piece of land which now pokes its head above the water is so flat that it is easy to imagine any shift in sea level would reclaim it for the undersea world. Only 3 miles long, at its widest Chrissi can only muster less than a mile. The most elevated spot is called Kefala or 'the head' but at fewer than 100 feet high it barely qualifies as a hill, although it provides a good vantage point to see the whole of the island. If the cedar trees are one of the main attractions on Chrissi, they are also its saviour. The intricate networks of their roots bind together the sands which are the very substance of its being.

Aristovoulos sweeps around the south coast of the island as the skipper confidently edges his ship bow first onto the small quay at Vougiou Mati. Hawsers are heaved ashore and looped round bollards and we are dispatched onto dry land. Some of our fellow passengers, eager to swim and soak up the sun, make a bee line for the umbrellas on the beach right by where our ship is moored.

Along with others we follow the sandy path which winds its way through the dunes and cedar trees. In less than ten minutes we have crossed to the north coast, to Chrissi's most renowned beach. Known as Belegrina, this golden sandy bay is washed by gin-clear water through which a seabed bejewelled with multi-coloured shells is revealed. This beach is touted as the nearest Greece comes to a Caribbean paradise. But could this be doing it an injustice?

Couldn't the boot be on the other foot and this be the beach by which others are judged? Whatever the case, its undoubted beauty has made it popular. Lines of reed umbrellas are soon providing shade and the small cantina serving refreshment for fellow travellers. Deciding to explore further west we stumble across the less popular beach of Hatzivolakas concealed in rocks surrounded by 250-year-old cedar trees.

The rockier seabed makes this an ideal place to snorkel. The varied environment is home to any number of colourful fish and the occasional octopus tending its garden of shells. Even at this time of year the sun is burning our backs and reluctantly we get out of the water to cover up with T shirts and sun cream. Deciding to explore further, our path takes us to a lonely white-walled chapel, baking in the midday sun, its pale blue roof lightly blending with the cloudless sky.

Peering into the darkness through the single window on the flank wall it is hard to see anything, and the church is locked. This is the chapel of Agios Nikolaos, believed to date from the 13th century when the Venetians held sway over Crete. By this time Chrissi had already seen its heyday, but to this day it displays evidence of former glories. Nearby there are Minoan ruins. Roman tombs and wells have also been unearthed. During the Byzantine period the islanders continued the tradition of their Minoan forebears and manufactured dye extracted from shells to colour the fine robes of royalty throughout Europe.

The dye, commonly known as Tyrian purple ('porphyra' in Greek), was extracted from sea snails, prevalent in the warm waters around the island. Its manufacture required many snails and was so labour intensive that it could only be afforded by the rich. During the Byzantine period its use was prohibited for colouring anything other than the robes of the imperial court. Any child of a Byzantine emperor was said to be 'born in the purple' or 'porphyrogenitos'.

Not far from the chapel an ancient salt pan is a relic of those Byzantine times. Before refrigeration, salt was a valuable commodity as a preservative and for centuries islanders would use it to trade with towns and villages on mainland Crete.

The demise of the Byzantine Empire left a power vacuum, soon filled by pirate gangs who seized the island, driving the fishermen and farmers who lived there back to the mainland. The geography of Chrissi made it an ideal base for the business of plundering. All trade travelling south of Crete would pass nearby and Chrissi's low-lying topography made it difficult for it to be spotted from any distance, while it was also far enough from the mainland for the brigands to make good their escape if subjected to raids from Crete.

The seas around here are littered with wrecks of ships which fell victims to piratical mischief. The Turks, determined to rid the island of this danger to their shipping, eventually prevailed. For centuries Chrissi then became the domain of shepherds who would bring their flocks to graze in winter, and fishermen who could draw their boats in close to the island to seek shelter when the harsh winds blew in from the west.

Chrissi is known to mainlanders in and around Ierapetra as simply 'the Island'. I suspect this is because, in the days when people didn't travel far from home, this was the only significant island they encountered. It is also known in some quarters as 'Gaidouronisi' or 'donkey island', from the word 'gaidaros'. Unfortunately we encounter no donkeys today, but have been told that elderly beasts used to be put out to pasture here when their working life was over.

Chrissi derives from the word meaning golden in Greek, and it is well named as much of the island is covered in sand. But this is not the whole story. The well-marked paths, which visitors are required to keep to, meander through golden dunes of coarse yellow sand sprouting juniper, thyme and cypresses as well as the renowned cedar trees. Much of the sand is red, however, and on some beaches almost white. Rocks the colour of henna, rust, oyster and leafy green litter the landscape. These boulders that have escaped the grinding and gnashing of the sea betray the island's volcanic origins, as do the wealth of fossils to be found, which are strictly protected. These are evidence of the volcanic eruption which created Chrissi, preserving organisms in ash and lava. Here they remained trapped until erosion of the rocks by the sea liberated them.

Close to the chapel on the west coast is an unmanned solar-powered lighthouse warning modern-day sailors of the shallow waters. We decide to explore to the east. At its furthest point we reach the beach at Kataprosopo. Meaning 'face to face', it is so called because it stares out on the island's smaller sibling of Micronisi, half a mile offshore. Looking across at this desolate islet, a haven for thousands of herring gulls that nest amongst its rocks, is like looking out over the edge of the world. From here, after Micronisi the sea stretches to infinity, there is no more land until Cyprus nearly 500 miles away, then Syria and the Middle East.

There is time for just one more swim before our ship sets sail so we stroll back to the beach at Vagies near the quay, managing to find an umbrella to sit under and enjoy a drink from the cantina.

Perfect Paleochora –
By Land and Sea

Paleochora has old world charm. It is also the perfect base for exploring south west Crete. Beauty abounds throughout its narrow streets, alive with busy cafes and tavernas among resplendent displays of potted plants bursting with every colour you can imagine. On this blessed promontory that reaches out into the lustrous Libyan Sea, you are never far from its beguiling waters. Sunsets here are as breathtaking as anywhere on the island and the hospitality shown by locals second to none.

Towards the end of the spit of land on which Paleochora stands are the unspectacular remains of a castle. It was the building of the fort in the 13th century which was largely responsible for the establishment of a settlement here, which grew up around the castle to service the needs of the incumbent Venetians.

The history of this fortification has been one of siege. Countless times was this citadel flattened and rebuilt. With no need for its defences now, it stands in some neglect on the margins of town but serves a new, unintentional purpose: as a shield hiding what might be considered a local folly.

At the end of the peninsula, the powers that be have built an extensive yacht marina. Mostly this lies empty, apart from the odd fishing vessel and forlorn pleasure boat. It is the height of the tourist season, and there is not one visiting yacht here. The ferries that tramp the south coast moor at the town quay near the tavernas and shops on the eastern side of town. The aura of the harbour is one that smacks of over-reached budgets.

The dusty tracks to the marina are largely unsigned and totally unmade, strewn with potholes. There are no waterside restaurants here and facilities are almost non-existent. The shame is, this could be a wonderful location and a boon to the local economy. For now it stands remote, its dusty quays and pontoons virtually devoid of craft.

It is here that we have come to board our dive boat which lies on its solitary mooring, stern in to the baking concrete jetty. This sun-bleached rib inflatable is to provide us access to the best offshore snorkelling sites. Kostas and Eva who run the trips greet us and we squeeze into wetsuits on the quayside. In this heat it is intensely uncomfortable but we will be grateful for them later on.

Masks, fins and safety briefing sorted we head through the harbour entrance, turning inside the passage between the headland and the rocky islet offshore. We are cruising parallel to the beach in the direction of our villa on the edge of the sands outside town.

At first the ride is smooth, the boat easily planing over the water, but Kostas has to throttle back as the waves get bigger and heavy spray washes over the boat. Conditions are deteriorating quickly. We take the decision to retrace our steps and head east back past Paleochora into the lee of its protective promontory.

Running with the sea astern we quickly round the headland and equilibrium is restored. More comfortably we set a course for the waters off beaches to the east of town.

Anchoring 200 yards offshore in 25 feet of water, rolling backwards off the floats, the sea is warm. Following Eva towing a marker buoy we keep close to our dive buddies. The seabed here is ideal for snorkelling as it undulates and changes constantly. Sand to rock then weed, in the diaphanous water sunlight illuminates what lies below.

Spiny urchins cling to rocks under which bashful octopus slither to their covert caves. Scorpion fish, menacing, lurk camouflaged above sandy beds, while shoals of rainbow wrasse and silver, flitting bream swim round us oblivious.

Stopping for a drink and biscuits back aboard, the tour takes us further east near rocks offshore of Anidri. Snorkelling here is dramatic; the rocks close to the surface and light good. A strong current means I have to keep my wits about me if I am not to drift too far from our guide. The sun getting lower, it is in my eyes and sometimes difficult to locate my dive buddy. The swim is exhilarating and challenging and after 50 minutes we hoist ourselves back aboard the rib. Whilst in the water, concentration and the spectacular sea life provide a welcome diversion to exertion. It is only when we return to the boat that tiredness hits. Sitting in the wind on the floats of the rib we are pleased to be wearing wetsuits.

To the west the sun is edging its way over the mountains skirting Paleochora, chased by the milky disc of a full moon rising behind us. We follow the sun towards harbour, unsure of the wisdom of plans to go dancing.

Veggera taverna lies right on the beach to the west of town. Tables and chairs populate a decking area giving way to the sands running down to the waters of the bay. A prime spot during daytime, Veggera panders to the needs of sun worshippers who enjoy the use of the taverna's loungers on the beach. Tonight, space on the terrace has been cleared and as we arrive musicians are setting up and doing their sound check. For those who have been snorkelling, tiredness is taking its toll and the prospect of activity daunting. But, ravenously hungry, we order food enough to cover the entire table. We devour mezedes of all sorts and as the band starts to play we feel restored.

The line-up consists a singer, lyra, laouto, fiddle and guitar and a woodwind player on whistle, recorder and bagpipes the like of which I have never encountered. The chanter is fairly traditional but the bag itself is made out of the skin of a wild boar. This is a modern-day version of one of the oldest Cretan instruments, the askomantoura. Originally fashioned by shepherds, the bag would have been made of the skin of a sheep, the wool trimmed but left on to stop it from bursting. The mouthpiece was carved from bone of the animal and the tuner whittled from wood, inside which reeds were encased that vibrate to make the bagpipe's distinctive sound.

The lyra is the beating heart of much traditional Cretan music. A three-stringed, pear-shaped instrument, it is played with a bow whilst held upright on the musician's knee. The laouto is similar to a lute, which usually has four paired strings and is strummed or picked like a guitar. From this heavenly pairing emanates a style of music which is unmistakably Cretan.

The musicians start their repertoire with folk songs, which they punctuate with conversation, cigarettes and raki. This is just a warm up. As our table empties of food, the seats around us fill with locals arriving for the evening's entertainment. Across the road inside the glass-fronted taverna we glimpse dancers in traditional costume. Laughing and chatting, five men and five women take the floor. The lead dancer is a giant of a man wearing black vraka, (wide breeches-style trousers) tucked into knee-length white boots. A white silk shirt beneath a black meidanogileko (waistcoat) trimmed with gold braid is finished off with a red sash tied around the waist on which an ornamental dagger is carried. His head sports a sariki (black fringed kerchief) of the type worn by many men in the mountain villages. The other male dancers wear a similar dress but in a royal blue colour.

The women wear long red skirts trimmed in gold, covered with embroidered white aprons. Long-sleeved blue or black velvet jackets with scooped necks reveal a bodice and red sash around the waist, all topped with red and gold kerchiefs. Some wear extravagant gold necklaces, others a simple crucifix. Such costumes date back to the 16th century. Although for women they are now kept for festivals, the men's attire is only a more formal version of what until recently would have been day-to-day clothes.

For the first dances the men and women take turns on the floor, the male dancers acrobatic and imperious, the women contained and proud. Typically the music starts slowly, the haunting melody of lyra rising and falling, gaining tempo, cajoling the dancers to greater feats of athletic prowess.

The jeopardy in the dancing is much increased by a tree with low hanging branches which stretches across the impromptu dance floor. This seems only to spur the dancer leading the line on, leaping as close to the branch as he can without bashing his head. Arms around each other's shoulders, the end of the line is held by the men in succession, starting with youngest, until the lead dancer steps up, leaping and slapping his heels, dipping and jumping as the music reaches a crescendo. This is the maleviziotis, which has roots in the traditional war dances of centuries ago, allowing for spectacular improvisation from the dancers.

It is hard for an Englishman not to feel such displays are put on purely for tourists but, rest assured, in Crete at least, these dances lie at the very heart of the culture. Dance tradition can be traced back to Minoan times, dance floors having been unearthed at the palace of Knossos. During the Hellenistic period, Cretans believed dancing was a way of talking to their Gods. Homer writes of the shield of Achilles bearing a picture of dancing at Knossos. The music is loved by old and young alike, and many children attend classes to learn the traditional dances of the island.

Now the men and women join together for the sousta, a dance of seduction. Starting in pairs the dancers promenade before making a circle. They separate and come together continuously throughout the dance before their final union. This sensual dance marks the end of the first half of the performance and the dancers leave the stage and head back to the restaurant for refreshment. Full with food and tired from diving we are too exhausted and enthralled to leave our seats. More drinks are ordered and we resign ourselves to a late night. Still, we have little to do tomorrow so can catch up on sleep. Anyway, we don't want to miss what the second part of the performance is likely to bring.

The dancers emerge in changed costumes. The men have ditched their sashes and waistcoats and are dressed all in black. The women have also gone for a less exotic look, now wearing long grey skirts and black tops, each with a chain and large gold crucifix around their necks.

The dancers approach tables, encouraging the reluctant audience to join them on the floor. One by one all but the most stubborn succumb and after the briefest demonstration of the moves we are off, a long uncontrolled line of laughing novices, would be experts and professional dancers, kicking and flicking its way around tables and onto the road. The traffic waits until we twist and turn our way back to the dance floor as the music stops.

A diffident few scuttle back to their chairs. Those who are enjoying themselves, or the undecided who hesitate too long, are soon caught up in the next number as the band strikes up. This time we are paired, circling and twirling and passing under human arches of hands, all the while urged on by the relentless lyra.

So the evening continues, we dance and dance until we can dance no more, and then we dance again. On the terrace, on the road and on the beach; even for the most inhibited amongst us the dancing is a joyful experience. If I had time to reflect it would be easy to see how fundamental such dancing is to Cretans, how it resonates with what it means to be the progeny of this island.

Way into the night the dancing continues. Any progress we are making in our proficiency is more than outweighed by exhaustion. Sitting out the occasional dance we make it through to the denouement, with just time for a night-cap to end this perfect day.

Around and About in Kritsa

Crossing the bridge over the canal on the Spinalonga Peninsula the early May sun is already blindingly bright. Reaching for sunglasses, I edge the car along the causeway, past the salt flats towards the main road. The sea is burnished, giving an inviting glimpse of the pleasures it holds for the day to come. I am heading inland on a short tour, starting with a place I have so far neglected to take in, before striking out to more familiar territory.

I cannot explain why I have not visited the Doric site of Lato. How many times must I have driven past the road that leads there on the way to my other destinations of Kritsa and Katharo. Such dereliction is inevitable when travelling around Crete; there is so much to see that it can never be exhausted. That is part of its allure.

Heading out of Elounda the familiar road traverses the peak which separates the fishing village from Agios

Nikolaos. This is one of the most picturesque drives on the island as you crest the top of the pass and look down across Mirabello. A cruise ship like a giant floating town dwarfs the quay to which it is tethered way beneath me. A lone yacht tacks its way towards the headland which leads to Spinalonga, leaving no memory of its passing on the ultramarine sea. Somewhat reluctantly I turn inland, skirting the back of the city, through the scrubland, abandoned lorries and filling stations which line the route to the National Highway.

Briefly I take this carriageway in the direction of Sitia, exiting at the town's newest and most confusing junction. It has been some years in the building, and my knowledge of its intricacies and dangers has grown alongside its construction, but for the uninitiated it is worth keeping your wits about you. With relief I turn onto the Kritsa road which winds its way up in the direction of what is reputed to be the island's largest village.

The turning for Lato is just as the road meets Kritsa, which makes it more inexplicable that I have not visited this ancient city to which Agios Nikolaos was a mere acolyte, the port region serving this capital on the hill. Perhaps it is the proliferation of Minoan settlements and their monumental archaeological significance that has overshadowed this site which, had it been anywhere else in the Greece, or for that matter the world, would come under more scrutiny. Even archaeologists appear to have neglected this town, not starting any major excavations until as recently as 1967.

The entrance to Lato is two-and-a-half miles up the road. It appears I am not alone in having disregarded the significance of this spot. The woman who takes my entrance fee is the only other being around. Selfishly, I am not disappointed. I have this whole ancient wonder to wander alone, and feel a sense of privilege that this island can bestow such an honour on me.

This city was built by the Dorians, although it is thought a smaller settlement predated their development on this land. What can be seen today dates from the 5th century BC, the remains of this city that survived until its destruction by earthquake around 200 BC. The ruins are substantial and the town's footprint can clearly be seen in the patterns made by the colossal stone blocks strewn on the mountainside.

Lato was built between two hills. From here lookouts could get a clear view all the way down to the sea at what is now Agios Nikolaos. The defence of this grand city was crucial and inside the walls can still be seen the remains of towers constructed to keep people safe in the event of attack from rival city states.

The nearest potential enemy was Olous, the sunken town which lies beneath the waters offshore of Elounda. For us the drive here had taken less than half an hour, but the long hike uphill would be exhausting for an attacking army, not only that but from this vantage point it would be totally exposed.

Just inside the main gate, in the shadows of the southern wall, are remains of warehouses, shops and workshops for pressing olives and milling flour, where citizens would go about their daily business. Opposite, beneath two of the fortress towers, lie what is left of the dwellings where people lived. Following a cobbled street as it steps up the hillside I reach the agora, the central open space that stood at the heart of communal affairs. To the north a flight of stone steps ascend to the prytaneion, or town hall. It was here that all civic decisions would have been taken. At the other end of the agora is a shrine to Artemis, for when townsfolk needed to appeal to a higher authority.

The name Lato is believed to have been derived from the name Leto, who was the mother of Artemis and Apollo. Often depicted as a hunter, Artemis was a wise deity to revere, as she had a wide brief. As well as being the goddess of animals, the hunt and nature, this immortal also presides over childbirth and protecting the virtue of young women. During the Classical Greek period the identities of Artemis and the midwife goddess Eileithyia become somewhat confused, and it is the face of the latter which appears minted on coins dug up in the city.

Her sibling Apollo was also worshipped here. The remains of a temple to the god can be seen on the southern hill above where I am standing. The agora is a wonderful social space. Here alone in the middle of this square, it is easy to imagine residents strolling the colonnaded portico of the stoa or sitting in the shade of a tree on stone benches discussing the minutiae of their lives or affairs of state. This city was the birthplace of Nearchus, Alexander the Great's friend, mentor and admiral of the fleet; was it sitting where I sit now that he dreamed dreams of his epic voyages of discovery?

This is a perfect spot, and its sublimity has not been missed by those who have chosen to live in the nearby village of Kritsa, which manages to achieve a blend of a thriving modern community without losing sight of its heritage. I retrace my steps to the main road as I am intent on revisiting the chapel of Panagia Kera to see its celebrated frescoes.

The design of the chapel, which is thought to emanate from the 13th century, is extraordinary. It is probably the additions built in the following 100 years that are culpable for its unique appearance. The neglect of any formal symmetry makes it all the more appealing and speaks of its chequered history.

The façade is shaped like three alpine peaks buttressed on either side. In the valley between the two right hand apexes nestles a solitary belfry. At the centre of the church is a dome, the inside of which is imbued with artwork which makes this church one of the most important religious sites on the island.

The trio of peaks on its exterior hint at the three barrel-vaulted aisles that are revealed on entering the chapel through the central portal. Although dark inside, on closer viewing every surface is ablaze with brightly-coloured frescoes. These restored Byzantine paintings depict any number of biblical scenes.

The central aisle is the oldest and dedicated to Mary, the mother of God, or Panagia. The two aisles that flank the original were added the following century and celebrate saints Anthony and Anne. The nave is decorated with four scenes from the life of Christ: the Presentation, the entry to Jerusalem, the Raising of Lazarus and, in the dome, the Baptism.

At one time the church is said to have housed an icon of the Virgin that possessed the power to work miracles. The original work was stolen during the Venetian occupation and taken to Italy but a new icon painted by an unknown artist in

1732 has taken its place. The number of paintings is overwhelming and however magnificent they may be, the sense is of the walls closing in on me. I escape the claustrophobic atmosphere, emerging outside into the light and head uphill to the main village.

Built into the side of the Dikti mountains, from above Kritsa resembles a scorpion. I have been told that planning regulations are in place to ensure it retains its unique outline. Whatever the truth of this, there is no sting in Kritsa's tail, it would be hard to find a more welcoming place.

Perched 1,300 feet above the sea, beneath the hill known locally as Kastellos, Kritsa has its roots in the Minoan era. On ancient paths that reach out from the village into the mountains beyond, are reminders of its heritage, with both Minoan and Doric artifacts having been discovered here. Kritsa's history has been turbulent, not least during Crete's fight for independence against the Ottoman invaders between 1669 and 1898. Time and again the Turks tried to lay waste this community and repeatedly the people rose up to resist and rebuild their birthright.

In the main square is a reminder of an act of heroism for which the village is best known. Here stands a statue to a woman called Rhodanthe, who is nowadays better known as Kritsotopoula. The story is well documented by local author Yvonne Payne in her fictionalised account of Rhodanthe's life, *Kritsotopoula: Girl of Kritsa,* who does it far more justice than I can here.

The book tells the true story of the daughter of the local priest who was abducted by a drunken Turkish soldier. Killing her mother in the assault he drags Rhodanthe off, imprisoning her in a house in the village. The soldier seeks to forcibly marry the girl, but during the night she slits his throat and escapes to the hills.

Cutting off her hair and binding her breasts she joins the resistance fighters disguised as a young man. Her identity remained secret until she was fatally injured in battle in 1823 and the truth was revealed. Visitors may notice a road running through the village is named after her. At the end of this street is a house with a cross carved above the door which was Rhodanthe's family home from where she was kidnapped.

Near Lato, on the spot she is believed to have been mortally wounded is another memorial to Kritsotopoula. Unveiled in 2009, this imposing life-size stone relief is the work of the sculptor and local resident Nigel Ratcliffe-Springall and was commissioned by the local villagers.

Such mementos of Kritsa's history are important, as standing here looking down the olive-draped valley to the sea it is hard to imagine such tempestuous times. Although thriving, Kritsa likes to take life at an easy pace as its streets wind their flower-adorned way into the Dikti Mountains. The blooms in perfect harmony with the embroidered and woven goods displayed outside shops alongside pottery, carved wood and leather goods.

I stop off to peruse the ceramics in the glass art workshop in the square before taking a seat to watch the world go by in a café. A priest sits for a smoke and a glass of raki while a man on a motorbike, a sheepdog riding pillion, stops for takeaway coffee. Walking uphill, shops give way to scenes of rural domesticity. Beneath arbours of bougainvillea, beside pots of geraniums, women dressed in black sit outside shelling peas, keeping half an eye on children playing on bikes in the alleys. I catch a few bars of Europop then some rembetika through windows thrown open against the heat. A motor scooter kicks up dust as its laughing rider talks into her mobile phone, cleverly navigating around a small cat asleep in the sun.

Understated yet beautiful, Kritsa forever downplays its allure. I could meander these streets endlessly and if ever I should tire of them I could take up the challenge of walking the little talked about gorge which runs 8 miles from north of the village, passing close by Lato to Tapes.

Today I am intent on taking another course, heading for Katharo Plain, a further 10 miles into the mountains along a road that twists and turns its way to 3,800 feet above sea level. I am following in the footsteps (although I am driving) of local shepherds who bring their flocks here to graze on the lush pastures, and farmers who only inhabit these highlands between May and October. During this time, Katharo is a land of plenty, but in winter it is a forbidding, often snowbound place, too harsh to support life.

Leaving Kritsa the road steeply saunters its way through olive groves interspersed with woods of cypresses, maple and holm oak. I feel the air cooling as I ascend, which is probably just as well as at times my car is not fond of the climb and I am concerned about it overheating. On several occasions I have to stop for goats which seem oblivious to the dangers of traffic. This is their world and rightly they are not to be rushed.

Near the summit, pulling off the road the silence is stunning, broken only by the buzzing of honey bees impatient to return to the multi-coloured hives which dot the landscape. The hillsides are a patchwork of apple and pear orchards, vineyards and arable land put over to growing cereals, potatoes and onions.

A lone Lammergeier vulture circles, riding the thermals above the mountain peaks, seeking out remains of dead animals on which to feast. It is not meat the bird is looking for but bones, from which the marrow provides the best part of its diet. These extraordinary creatures have developed the technique of carrying large bones up to 500 feet into the air and dropping them on rocks so they shatter, exposing the marrow inside.

At this time of year the plain is dazzling with wildflowers, a carpet of yellow, dotted with red poppies, white daisies and purple campanulas. It seems appropriate that these 'bellflowers' thrive here, the shape of their blooms a silent echo of the tinkling goat bells which play a symphony to the slopes on which the flocks graze.

I am hoping to get lunch at the extraordinary Zervas Taverna. It is some time since I have been this way and don't know if it is still open. I needn't have worried and the owners are as welcoming as I remember them to be. This taverna is fascinating, the walls covered in pictures of the plateau and its wildlife. This place it was that I first heard the story of the dwarf hippopotamus and elephants which roamed here during the mid-Pleistocene period. Sceptical at first, it was only when I saw the collection of fossils from Katharo in the Natural History Museum in Heraklion that I was fully convinced I wasn't being spun a line.

It is not known exactly how these non-indigenous creatures ended up on Crete. One theory is that in the Ice Age of 540,000 years ago distances between land masses were significantly reduced by frozen seas and giant ice flows. During this period it is thought that several of each species managed to make the journey to Crete and start breeding. They were not originally dwarf animals, and initially without any natural predators, they flourished. However, as the populations expanded, food supplies dwindled and the species evolved by growing smaller. From bones discovered, the hippos are believed to have been the size of a sheep and the elephants no larger than a cow.

Just as an Ice Age was thought to have enabled these extraordinary animals to establish themselves, another later Ice Age, 100,000 years ago, led to their demise. Around this time deer migrated to the island. Being more agile they were better adapted to surviving off the dwindling food supplies. Sadly, life became unsustainable for the dwarf hippos and elephants.

Nowadays the wildlife may be considered less exotic, but if you keep your wits about you, as well as the Lammergeier vultures it is possible to see griffon vultures, golden eagles, and any number of lizards and snakes, which I do not get close enough to identify, although I am assured the reptiles on Crete are of no threat to humans.

The plain is compact, being about 4 miles long and only a mile wide, and is owned communally by the people of Kritsa. Farmers who use the land pay a small percentage of the income from their produce back to the community. There is no mains electricity, generators providing any power required. In past times villagers would remain on the plain throughout summer, but improved roads and transport mean they can now return to Kritsa or take produce to market in Agios Nikolaos whenever they need to.

Before I follow that same route I sit down in Zervas Taverna to a potato omelette accompanied by a salad bursting with juicy tomatoes, plump olives and salty, crumbling feta and a plate of dakos (dried rusks) accompanied by freshly-squeezed orange juice. I suspect that nothing on my plate came from more than within a mile radius of the taverna, which couldn't make me happier.

Home Again?

The rain brushes the rooftops of the village. Across the olive groves all the way down to the bay, the water bleeds colour, blurring the edges of sea and sky. Below, through a nebula of blended hues, I can just make out the canal linking the Gulf of Korfos to neighbouring Mirabello and the villas on Kalydon where we so often stay. The sun parts the cloud, lifting the gauze, instantly infusing the scene with light and the world is new again.

From the roof terrace of this old stone house in Epano Elounda is painted the most perfect image that I can imagine. Even in the rain the richness of the vista remains undiminished. Is it on this very spot, in this tiny village on a mountainside just above Elounda, that our search will end? If Crete feels like my spiritual home, then just here feels the very quintessence of that and I hope it may become our physical home.

We have loved this tiny village since visiting some years ago to see the set built for the filming of Victoria Hislop's novel *The Island* for television. Alongside the small stone houses were built facades of buildings that looked so real we had to knock on the walls to distinguish the authentic buildings from the facsimiles. The film set is now gone and the village has returned to sleepy normality, the real island of Spinalonga floating in the distance between the figs, vines and olive trees which tumble down the mountain to the sea.

This village has a church and a single taverna which only opens at weekends, but it is a short drive from Elounda, and only a 20 minute walk from the coast. For us it will be a perfect place to write and relax and as a base to explore more of hidden Crete.

Walking through the deserted village streets we are invited in to the house of an elderly lady with piercing blue eyes. Her house is a makeshift kafenio and she cuts up apple which she proffers along with a glass of raki. She has seen us looking at the house and with a mixture of gestures and halting Greek we communicate we hope to buy it. She seems pleased, and we sit for some time in faltering conversation punctuated by long, content silences.

Saying goodbye to our new friend, we find the sun has already dried the paths and set free the intense aromas of mountain herbs and vibrant flowers bursting from pots and patches of earth around the village. We wander, making plans to the endless accompaniment of cicadas rasping their songs of love. I hope we will return here soon to somewhere we can call home.

Extract from Hidden Crete –

A Notebook

I am shaken awake by the wind beating on the unsecured shutter of the apartment window as the thunder rolls in from the Libyan Sea. Just hours earlier, I was sitting on the balcony reading, beneath a sky of stars glinting like celestial buoys, laid to navigate its infinite expanse to eternity. Now waves crash on the beach below and I am minded of Joni Mitchell's homage to Matala, just 30 miles eastwards.

'The wind is in from Africa, last night I couldn't sleep…'

The words of her song *Carey* roll around in my head like the storm bouncing off the White Mountains inland, until tiredness takes me.

I come round to a silence broken only by the sound of chairs and tables being rearranged in the taverna downstairs.

I open the shutters to a sky washed clear blue by the rain and tumble-dried by the hot sorokos of the night. The sea has resumed its calm demeanour, the only vestiges of storm a mere ripple that gently sucks and blows at the sands below.

A fishing boat putters its way across the bay, steering a course we hope to follow later when we head the 3 nautical miles along the coast to Loutro.

It has been some 30 years since I was last here in Chora Sfakion, and little has changed. Only tens of miles distant as the eagle flies from the northern coast of Crete, Chora Sfakion is a world away in essence. It is truly part of a hidden Crete. Places like this isolated outpost make travelling through this island's mystical landscape a serendipitous experience that is impossible to exhaust.

Here we are, perched on the edge of Europe. The isle of Gavdos, 25 miles due south, is the most southerly part of the continent. To the east on this same coast is Ierapetra, the most southern city in Europe. We are in border territory. Crete, an accident of a violent volcanic birth, stands poised on the margins of Europe, Asia and Africa, which endows this island with its cosmopolitan cultural legacy and turbulent history.

Anchored in an area of perpetual tectonic activity, Crete's geographical location also exposes it to extreme heat during summer and lays it open to strong winds throughout the year. Its strategically advantageous position in the Mediterranean has brought it the unwanted attentions of any number of foreign armies and pirates through the ages. It is these factors that have shaped Crete's contrasting and endlessly intriguing landscape and culture.

Inhabitants of this largest island in the Greek archipelago, although fiercely loyal to Greece, see themselves as Cretans first and Greeks second. It is worth remembering that, although Crete is considered by many to be the cradle of European civilisation, for much of its tempestuous past it came under the yoke of foreign powers. It was as recently as 1913 that Crete became part of the newly independent Greece.

Since then Crete has been ravaged by German occupation during the Second World War, the Greek Civil War that followed, and the military dictatorship between 1967 and 1974. Being estranged from the motherland for such long periods led Crete to establish unique traditions and customs. Its dialect has the harsh edge of many of its wines. The food served up is honest and unadorned, a reflection of the people, who are open and generous and wear their hearts on their sleeves.

From this piece of rock no more than 160 miles long and, at its widest point 38 miles across, emanated many civilising concepts that we, in our modern democratic societies, take for granted.

The limestone mountain ranges of Levka Ori, Psiloritis, Dikti and Sitia dominate the landscape inland but among them nestle fertile plains and prodigious ravines carved out by millennia of gushing mountain springs.

The seas that wash these shores can change their humour in an instant – one minute benign, the next enraged – sending fishing boats scampering for the safety of harbour. And all this is illuminated by the most lustrous light that renders any attempt to define it inadequate.

As we stroll past the memorial commemorating those who died in the evacuation of allied troops from Chora Sfakion to Egypt following the Battle of Crete in 1941 our ferry, the blue-hulled *Neptune*, makes its way into harbour. Could it be the same boat I travelled on from Agia Roumeli when I last visited all those years ago? Surely that was white? Is my memory deserting me? As the lines are thrown ashore and the boat is drawn towards the quayside I notice chips in its dark blue paintwork revealing white beneath the blue. The layers of paint so deep that, like the rings in a tree trunk, they betray the many years served by this trusty workhorse.

Although I visit Crete regularly, this time is more than ever a journey of discovery, revisiting places that I fondly remember and discovering new places that are off the beaten track. I have called this book *Hidden Crete* in the full knowledge that in these days of mass tourism and improved transport links there are few places that remain undiscovered. For seasoned visitors to the island many of these places are not hidden at all. Some mentioned are in familiar spots but may just be overlooked, hiding in the shadows of more popular nearby destinations. The places that I visit in this book are best defined as those that are not top of the list for first-time travellers to the island, that might be missed, and could prove a worthwhile diversion to those with a more adventurous spirit or inquisitive nature. Of course there are many worthwhile spots that are not mentioned here, either because there is no space or because I have not discovered these places myself. Part of the charm of Crete is its ability to astound the traveller by always revealing something new.

We sit aft, on the starboard side of the cockpit. From this vantage point we can watch the coast pass as we head west. Astern the blue and white of the Greek ensign flies proudly from its staff, reflective of the sea and sky, its nine blue and white stripes symbolizing the number of syllables in those three words, *elefteria i thanatos*, (freedom or death), which so embody the spirit of the Cretan people.

All life is here on the boat: a few early-season German tourists, a priest in his grey robes holding on to his kalimavkion stovepipe hat to stop it blowing out to sea, deliverymen with supplies for the tavernas and hotels, itinerant workers on their way to their daytime shift and families on a day out or visiting relatives. Excitable chatter almost drowns out the bass notes of the thudding engines as we coast past the spectacular sweet water (Glyka Nero) beach, a line of stunted trees growing out of the pebbles beneath the vertiginous foothills of the White Mountains, only accessible by boat or on foot via a steep path.

On the western end of the beach there is a small taverna built over the waves where water taxis can stop and deposit their fares. There are a few early sunbathers on loungers, but other than that the beach is quiet. The last time I visited here was by kayak from Loutro. The water washing the beach is unusually cold as it emanates from icy freshwater springs that bubble up from underground and mingle with the Libyan Sea.

We plough on, our wake the only furrow breaking the surface of a mercury sea, a lone chapel perched on the cliffside the sole mark of man now visible on the rugged shoreline. A few minutes later and Loutro reveals itself, clinging to the stark backdrop of mountains but turned to face the sparkling blue waters from which we now approach.

The only natural harbour on the south coast of Crete, it is crescent-shaped, with tavernas and bars lining the narrow pebble beach. A few fishing boats and a caique bob on moorings in the bay as the bow wave of our ferry passes. We turn inshore of a small island with its lighthouse guarding the western approaches and the captain eases his vessel alongside the quay.

Surprisingly, for a place that is not accessible by car, there is a refuse lorry on the dock. I later learn it comes over on the larger car ferry, the bins from the village are emptied into it before the truck returns to Chora Sfakion and is driven away to deposit its rubbish elsewhere. As we disembark and our fellow passengers disperse to go about their business, the engine is cut and the silence is deafening.

To come here is to get a sense of isolation. If Crete itself eases the stresses of daily life, Loutro wipes them away. Even today, when Greece is in the grip of a financial crisis that continues to threaten its very future, for the visitor at least those worries seem a million miles away and for locals, too, such concerns appear more diluted than on the mainland and in the large cities. Perhaps this has to do with the knowledge that, of all the islands, despite garnering a significant amount of income from tourism, Crete would be able to sustain its population through agriculture. Crops of olives and grapes are supplemented by fruit orchards and market gardens; multi-coloured hives store the honey of millions of bees; sheep and goats graze the mountainsides; and fishing boats take to sea from the smallest of harbours.

The Cretans take comfort in the knowledge that these age-old resources are plenty to sustain the indigenous population of some 600,000 people, of which only half live in the urban centres, mostly situated along the northern coast. Although the climate can be one of extremes, with summer temperatures frequently in the mid 30s and snow covering the high plateaux and mountains for much of the winter, the fertile soils provide a wealth of the healthiest produce.

As I am sitting at a taverna right on the Loutro seafront sipping a cold Mythos beer, another larger vessel makes its mooring. This car ferry plies the route between Chora Sfakion, Agia Roumeli and Paleochora. Called *Daskalogiannis,* it shares its name with the international airport at Chania.

I recall the story of Yannis Vlachos, who is seen by Cretans to have typified the Sfakian qualities of unflinching bravery and patriotism. He was nicknamed John the Teacher or Daskalogiannis because he was considered to be wise. Born to a well-to-do merchant in the 18th century, he grew up to become a wealthy ship owner and chairman of the local council of Sfakia.

During the Cretan revolt in 1770 he led a force of local palikars against the ruling Turks, liberating much of the region around Chora Sfakion, and was promised support from the seemingly sympathetic Russians. The flag of freedom was raised above the church in Anopolis, Vlachos' birthplace. Coins were even minted by the newly free region and put into local circulation. But the Russians reneged on their promise and, with help failing to materialise, Vlachos' troops could hold out no longer against the vastly greater numbers of Turks. His ragtag army finally surrendered at Frangokastello Castle several miles to the east of Chora Sfakion. Daskalogiannis was taken to Heraklion, where he was tortured then skinned alive in public in front of the harbour fort. He bravely bore his fate in silence, his demise witnessed by his brother who was forced to watch, an event that is believed to have sent him mad.

Sitting here in the peace of this isolated bay, as the ship honouring a Sfakiot hero discharges its straggle of passengers, it is hard to imagine those violent times. But scratch the surface of this magical island almost anywhere and a tale of struggle, myth or of great historical importance emerges, imbuing the present with the significance of the past. It is here, in places like Sfakia, that hidden Crete gives up its secrets.

Get by in Greek

The following words and phrases are intended to give you a start at getting by in Greek. Use these, and your attempts at speaking the language will always be appreciated. The spellings used below are as close an approximation of words written in the Greek alphabet as I can get, as frequently no exact transliteration is possible. Dive in and have a go, a little Greek can go a long way…

Greetings and courtesies

Hello *Yasas*

Goodbye *Adio*

Good morning *Kalimera*

Good evening *Kalispera*

Good night *Kalinichta*

Please/You're welcome *Parakalo*

Thank you *Efheristo*

OK *Endaxi*

Sorry *Signomi*

I don't understand *Then katalaveno*

Cheers *Issyia/Yamas*

Questions and Answers

Yes *Ne*

No *Ochi*

Where is? *Poo eene?*

How much is? *Poso kani?*

What is this? *Ti ine afto?*

Do you speak English? *Milate Anglika?*

What's your name? *Pos sas lene?*

What's the time? *Ti ora eene?*

How are you? *Ti kanete?*

Very well *Poli kala*

Not too bad *Etsi ketsi*

Not very well *Ochi ke toso kala*

My name is Richard *Me lene Richard*

Weather

It's hot *Ti zesti*

It's cold *Ti krio*

Numbers

One *Ena*

Two *Dio*

Three *Tria*

Four *Tessera*

Five *Pende*

Six *Exi*

Seven *Efta*

Eight *Octo*

Nine *Enya*

Ten *Deka*

Fractions

Half *Miso*

Quarter *Tetarto*

Weights and Measures

Litre *Litro*

Kilo *Kilo*

Gram *Gramario*

In the Taverna

I'd like *Tha ithela*

Could I have the bill please? *To logorizmo parakalo?*

Drinks

Beer *Bira*
Coffee *Kafe*
Juice *Himos*
Lemonade *Limonada*
Tea *Tsai*
Water *Nero*
Wine *Krasi*

Food

Beef *Vodino kreas*
Bread *Psomi*
Butter *Vootiro*
Cheese *Tiri*
Chicken *Kotopolo*
Eggs *Avga*
Fish *Psari*
Fruit *Froota*
Ham *Zambon*
Lamb *Arni*
Meat *Kreas*
Milk *Ghala*
Pork *Hirinio*
Potato *Patata*
Salad *Salada*
Steak *Brizola*
Sugar *Zachari*
Vegetables *Lachanika*

Useful words

Airport *Airodromio*

Bank *Trapeza*

Bad *Kakos*

Big *Megalo*

Bus stop *Stasi*

Car *Aftokinito*

Church *Eklisia*

Come here/in *Ella*

Doctor *Iatros*

Garage *Garaz*

Hospital *Nosokomio*

Let's go *Parme*

Little *Ligo*

Mobile phone *Kinito*

Petrol *Venzini*

Petrol station *Venzinathiko*

Pharmacy *Pharmakio*

Photograph *Photographia*

Postbox *Gramatokivotio*

Postcard *Kart postal*

Rain *Vrochi*

Room *Thomatio*

School *Skolio*

Shower *Doosh*

Stamps *Gramatosima*

Sun *Ilios*

Ticket *Isitirio*

Today *Simera*

Toilet *Toiluata*

Tomorrow *Avrio*

Tonight *Apopse*

Wait *Perimene*

Well *Kala*

The History of Crete At-a-Glance

Here is a brief synopsis of the major events in Greek history. For some of the ancient history the dates are approximate, as exact dates in many cases have not been established.

7000 BC Neolithic Period

2800 BC Early Helladic Bronze Age civilization, Greek mainland

2700 BC Minoan Bronze Age, Crete

1900 BC Minoan Palaces built on Crete, including Knossos.

1800 BC Proto-Greek speaking tribes, forerunners of the Mycenaeans, arrive on Greek mainland.

1700 BC Earthquake destroys Minoan palaces on Crete. New palaces and towns rebuilt.

1400 BC Minoan civilisation destroyed by invasion of Mycenaeans on Crete.

1200 BC The Trojan Wars.

1100 BC Fall of the Mycenaeans displaced by Dorian Greeks.

750 BC Homer writes *The Iliad* followed 20 years later by *The Odyssey*.

505 BC Democracy introduced in Athens, making way for the Classical Greek period.

384 BC Birth of Aristotle.

356 BC Birth of Alexander the Great.

323 BC Alexander the Great dies, Hellenistic period begins.

67 BC Romans conquer Crete.

33 AD Crucifixion of Christ.

286 AD Roman Empire divides into East and West creating the Byzantine Empire.

1204 AD Fourth Crusade leaves Byzantine Empire in disarray. Crete awarded to the Italian crusader leader Prince Boniface who sells it to the Venetians.

1645 AD Ottoman Turks capture Chania on Crete.

1669 AD Candia (Heraklion) on Crete surrenders to the Turks, Venetian presence on the island ends.

1821 AD Greek revolution and declaration of independence, although this is not fully achieved for another eight years.

1832 AD Prince Otto installed as King of Greece (at this time the Peloponnese, Athens, the Mani and the islands of the Saronic Gulf, Cyclades and Sporades).

1841 AD Cretan Revolt quashed by Ottoman Turks.

1858 AD Cretan Revolt secures right to carry arms and the equality of worship.

1866 AD The Great Cretan Revolt wins sympathy abroad and some concessions, but is ultimately quashed and by 1869 Crete is back under Ottoman control.

1878 AD Under the Pact of Halepa, Crete becomes a semi-independent state still within the Ottoman Empire.

1889 AD Halepa Pact collapses and Turkey sends troops and re-establishes martial law on Crete, but their violent actions lead to sympathy abroad for the Cretan cause.

1897 AD Cretan revolt leads to the 'Great Powers' of Britain, France, Italy and Russia taking over governance of Crete.

1898 AD Independent Cretan state governed by Prince George of Greece founded.

1908 AD Cretan deputies unofficially declare union with Greece.

1913 AD Following Balkan War Crete becomes part of independent Greece.

1923 AD Greco-Turkish population exchange, West Thrace becomes part of independent Greece.

1939 AD Start of Second World War.

1940 AD Following 'Ochi Day' Greece is invaded by the Axis powers.

1941 AD Crete falls to Axis powers.

1944 AD Start of Greek Civil War.

1949 AD Greek Civil War ends.

1952 AD Greece joins NATO.

1967 AD Coup of the Colonels.

1974 AD Cyprus crisis, collapse of the military dictatorship.

1975 AD New republican constitution becomes law.

1981 AD Greece joins European Community.

2009 AD Debt crisis plunges Greece into civil unrest.

Greek Food At-a-Glance

The following list is by no means exhaustive but I hope it gives a flavour of the foods on offer in Crete.

Appetizers, Starters and Mezedes

Dolmades Stuffed vine leaves

Sardeles pastes Salted sardines

Gavros marinates Anchovies in oil, lemon and herbs

Saginaki Deep fried cheese

Saginaki garides Shrimp with cheese and tomato sauce

Revithia-keftedes Deep fried chickpea balls

Tsatsiki Yoghurt, cucumber and garlic sauce

Taramasalata Blended fish roe, oil and lemon salad

Kolokythokeftedes Fried courgette balls

Tyrokeftedes Fried cheese balls

Boksades Lamb cubes with feta cheese in pastry

Spanakopita Spinach pie

Tyropita Feta cheese pie

Skordalia Garlic, potato and lemon sauce

Fava Split pea, garlic and lemon sauce

Salads

Horiatiki salata (Greek country salad) Tomatoes, onion, cucumber, feta cheese and olives

Ampelofasoula salata String bean, tomato and olive salad

Patatasalata Potato, onion, parsley and olive salad

Lahanosalata Cabbage, carrot, garlic and lemon juice salad

Garidosalata Shrimp salad

Meat Dishes

Mousaka Aubergines, mince, potatoes and béchamel sauce

Kotopolo me patates sto fourno Roast chicken and potatoes

Arni me patatas sto forno Roast lamb and potatoes

Souvlaki Grilled meat, usually lamb or chicken on skewers with peppers, onions and tomatoes

Gyros pitta Sliced grilled lamb served in pitta bread with salad and tsatsiki

Sofrito Veal with wine, garlic and parsley sauce

Kleftiko Slow-cooked lamb with potatoes, garlic, oil and lemon juice

Paidakia Grilled lamb chops

Keftedes Deep fried meatballs

Macaroni me kima Pasta with minced beef, garlic and onion

Beefteaki Seasoned minced beef patty

Sousoukakia Seasoned, grilled minced-beef balls in tomato sauce

Brizole Steak

Pastisada Veal, tomato and onion stew with spaghetti

Tomates gemistes Tomatoes stuffed with minced beef and onions

Moschari stifado Veal stew with tomatoes and onions

Kotopolo me portokali Slow-cooked chicken in orange juice

Gemista Baked peppers and tomatoes stuffed with rice and herbs

Saligaria me ryzi Fried snails with rice

Fish Dishes

Garides Shrimps

Mydia Mussels

Barbounia Red mullet

Ksifias Swordfish

Gavros Anchovy

Kalimari Squid

Astakos Lobster

Kolioi Mackerel

Bakaliaros Cod

Maridaki Whitebait

Sardeles Sardines

Tonos Tuna

Psarasoupa Fish soup

Psari plaki Baked fish

Puddings and Pastries

Loukoumades Deep fried dough balls with honey and cinnamon

Pastelli Honey and walnut wafers

Amydalopi Almond cake

Baklava Filo pastry with cinnamon, walnuts and honey

Kataifi Almond and walnut pastry with syrup

Yaourti me meli Yoghurt and honey

Rizogalo Rice pudding

About the Author

Richard Clark is a writer, editor and journalist who has worked on an array of national newspapers and magazines in the UK. In 1982, on a whim, he decided to up sticks and go and live on the Greek island of Crete. So began a love affair that has continued to this day, when he still visits the Greek islands, where he has a home, on a regular basis. In 2016 he gave up the daily commute to London to become a full-time author. He is married with two grown up children and a granddaughter, and lives in Kent.

Did You Enjoy this Book?

If you liked reading this book and have time, any review on www.amazon.com or amazon.co.uk would be appreciated, and it would be good to meet up with any readers on facebook at www.facebook.com/richardclarkbooks.

Printed in Great Britain
by Amazon